Journey for Myself

Colette

Journey for Myself

SELFISH MEMORIES

TRANSLATED FROM THE FRENCH BY
DAVID LE VAY

PETER OWEN · LONDON

ISBN 0 7206 0430 3

Translated from the French and selected from
Oeuvres Complètes de Colette, Vol. VI (*Le Voyage
Egoïste* and *Aventures Quotidiennes*)

VH 9 7

PETER OWEN LIMITED
12 Kendrick Mews Kendrick Place London SW7

First British Commonwealth edition 1971
English translation © 1971 Peter Owen
© 1949 Le Fleuron, Paris

Printed in Great Britain by
A. Wheaton & Co Exeter

Preface

The first four essays in this volume—*Sunday, I'm Hot, Respite* and *Invalid*—originally appeared in *La Chambre Éclairée*. They were first collected for publication, together with a number of other essays from the same and other sources and entitled *Le Voyage Égoïste*, under the signature of Colette Willy in a *de luxe* edition illustrated by coloured lithographs issued by Éditions d'Art Édouard Pelletan in 1922.

In 1928 Ferenczi, using the same title, published the four essays named above and included a group of fashion articles written by Colette for *Vogue* between 1925 and 1927; the latter were accorded the subtitle *Quatre Saisons*.

At about the same time a dozen of these later essays of Colette were privately published by Philippe Ortiz for his friends in a volume also entitled *Quatre Saisons*. But the rest of this volume included the last group of essays, the *Aventures Quotidiennes*, which did not appear in any generally published version until their inclusion in the *Oeuvres Complètes* of the Le Fleuron edition of 1949, from which they are now translated for the first time.

The publishers of the present volume wish to express their gratitude to Monsieur Maurice Goudeket for his help in making available for translation some of this material, and also for lending various personal photographs of Colette.

Contents

Everyday Adventures

Illustrations

Journey for Myself

Sunday

What's the matter with you? Don't bother to answer 'Nothing', bravely screwing up your features; the next moment the corners of your mouth fall again, your eyelids droop over your eyes, and your chin is really regrettable. *I* know what's the matter with you.

Your trouble is that it's Sunday, and raining. If you were a woman you'd burst into tears because it's raining and it's Sunday, but you're a man and you daren't. You lend an ear to the sound of the fine rain—the trickling sound of thirsty sand—despite yourself you contemplate the glistening street and the mournful closed shops, and you take a grip on your poor masculine nerves, you hum a little tune, light a cigarette which you forget and which goes out in your dangling fingers. . . .

I'd really rather wait till you've had enough and come to me for help. . . . You think that's malicious? No, it's just that I'm so fond of your childish way of stretching out your arms to me and dropping your head on my shoulder as if you were giving it to me for keeps. But it's raining so gloomily and it's so Sundayish today that, even before you ask, I make the three magic passes : draw the curtains, light the lamp, and arrange on the divan, among your favourite cushions, my shoulder, hollowed for your cheek, and my arm ready to encircle your neck.

Is it nice like this? Not yet? Lie quiet then, wait for our shared animal warmth to penetrate the cushions. Slowly the silk loses its chill under my cheek, under my back, your head gradually sinks on my shoulder and your whole body becomes heavy and limp beside me and spreads out as if you were melting. . . .

Don't say anything : I can hear your great shuddering sighs better than words. . . . You hold your breath, you're afraid your sigh may end in tears. Ah, if only you dared. . . .

There, I've thrown my blue scarf over the lamp; across the stems of a tall bunch of chrysanthemums you can barely see the firelight dancing; stay there in the shadow, forget that I'm your lover, forget how old you are and even that I'm a woman, relish

15

the humiliation and the pleasure—because it's a desolate November Sunday, because it's cold and raining heavily—of once more becoming a nervous child who returns irresistibly and innocently to female warmth, undemanding save for the living shelter and the still caress of two encircling arms.

Stay there. You're back in the cradle; you want a magic song or story . . . I don't know any stories. And I shan't invent the happy story of a fairy princess who loves a magician-prince, even for you. For there's no place for love in the heart you have now, in your orphan's heart.

I don't know any stories. . . . Isn't it enough if I whisper in your ear? Give me your hand, grasp mine firmly; it will take you back, without stirring, to those humble Sundays I used to love so much. Here we are, hand in hand, getting smaller and smaller, on the steel-blue road glinting with metallic flints—it's a road in my own part of the world. . . .

I lead you quietly, as you're only a nice Parisian child, and as we walk I look at your white hand in my small brown paw, dry with cold and reddened to the finger-tips. My little peasant's hand, it looks like one of the leaves that linger in the hedgerow, lit up by autumn. . . .

The steel-coloured road bends here, so sharply that we stop in surprise at an unexpected village. . . . My God, I lead you religiously towards my old home, you small, well-mannered, unastonished child, and all you can say while I tremble on my regained threshold is : 'It's only an old house . . .'

Come in. Let me explain. First, you can tell it's Sunday by the smell of the chocolate that dilates your nostrils, sweetens the throat deliciously. . . . See, when you wake up and breathe the warm smell of boiling chocolate, you know it's Sunday. You know that at ten o'clock there will be cracked pink cups on the table, and flaky girdle-cakes—here, see, in the dining-room—and that it's all right to go without the big midday meal. . . . Why? I couldn't say. . . . That's how it was when I was a child.

Don't cast up your eyes so timidly at the dark ceiling. Everything in this house takes care of you. It has so many wonderful things! This blue Chinese vase, for instance, and this deep window recess where the falling curtain hides me completely. . . .

You say nothing? Oh! little boy, I show you a magic vase whose belly mutters with imprisoned dreams, the enchanted grotto where I immure myself with my favourite ghosts, and you stay unmoved, disappointed, your hand doesn't even tremble in mine? After that I hardly risk taking you into my bedroom, where the mirror is draped with grey lacework, more delicate than a veil of hair, spun by a great spider that's come in from the garden, sensitive to the cold.

It watches from the middle of its web and I don't want you to be frightened of it. Lean over the mirror; our two children's faces, yours pale, mine scarlet, smile through the double lattice. . . . Don't stop by the commonplace little white bed, rather by the wooden judas-window that pierces the wall; it's there the straying cat enters at dawn—she flops on my bed, cold, white and light like an armful of snow, and goes to sleep on my feet. . . .

You still don't smile, my sophisticated little friend. But I've kept the garden to win you over. As soon as I open the worn door, as soon as the two rickety steps have given under our feet, can't you scent a fragrance of soil, of walnut leaves, of chrysanthemums and smoke? You sniff like an untrained dog, you shiver. . . . The sour smell of a garden in November, the gripping Sunday silence of the woods, abandoned by the woodcutter and his cart, the sodden forest path where a strand of mist moves languidly, all this is ours till evening if you wish, as it's Sunday.

But perhaps you prefer my last, my most haunted domain—the ancient hayloft, vaulted like a church. Inhale with me the floating dust of the old embalmed hay that tickles like a fine snuff. Our sudden sneezes will stir up a whole crowd of silvery rats, of thin, half-wild cats; bats will fly for a moment in the ray of blue daylight that transfixes the velvet shadow from roof to floor. . . . Now you'll have to grasp my hand and hide your head, glossy and black as a well-groomed kitten—under my long hair. . . .

Can you still hear me? No, you're asleep. I'd like to keep your heavy head on my arm and listen to you sleeping. But I'm a little jealous. Because it seems to me, seeing you unconscious there with your eyes closed, that you've stayed back there, in my very old country garden, and that your hand is still clinging to the rough little hand of a child who looks like me. . . .

I'm Hot

Don't touch me. I'm hot! . . . Keep away from me! But don't just stand there in the doorway, you're blocking, you're stealing from me the slight breeze that struggles from window to door like a clumsy, imprisoned bird. . . .

I'm hot . . . I can't sleep. I contemplate the dark atmosphere of my sealed-up room, where a golden rake with equal teeth moves and slowly, slowly combs the smooth lawn of the carpet. When the striped shadow of the shutters reaches my bed, I'll get up—perhaps . . . till then I'm hot.

I'm hot. The heat engulfs me like an illness, like a passion. It's enough to fill every hour of the day and night. I can't talk of anything else; I complain of it passionately, and meekly, this pitiless caress. See! That's what's given me this glaring mark on my chin and has slapped my face, and I can't rid my hands of the gauntlets, the colour of brown bread, that it's drawn on my skin. And this fistful of golden specks, all on fire, that have sanded my face, it's that, it's that again. . . .

No, don't go down into the garden, you bother me. The gravel will crunch under your feet, I'll think you're crushing a bed of cinders. Quiet! I can hear the fountain playing feebly—it's going to run dry—and the panting of the dog stretched on the hot stone. Don't move! I've been waiting since morning under the limp aristolochia leaves, hanging like hides, for the first breath of wind to stir. Oh, I'm hot! Ah! Listen, there's the silky noise, like a fan opening and closing, of a pigeon flying round the house!

I can't stand any longer this thin, crumpled sheet that was so grateful to my bare heels earlier. But at the end of my room there's a mirror, all blue with shadow, ruffled with reflections. . . .

How tempting and cold the water is!

Imagine you're seeing yourself in it, the water of the lakes where I come from! They slumber in summertime, warm here, made icy there by the upsurge of a deep spring. They are opaque and bluish, with treacherous inhabitants; the water-snake there twines round the long stalks of the water-lilies and the arrow-heads. . . . They smell of reeds, of musky mud, green hemp. . . . Bring me their coolness, their fever-cradling mists, so that I shiver. I'm so hot. . . .

Or else give me—but you won't—just a small piece of ice in the hollow of my ear and another there on my arm, in the bend of the elbow. . . . You don't want to? You let me ask in vain, you're so tiresome. . . .

Do take a look and see if the daylight is beginning to change colour, if the dazzling stripes of the shutters are becoming blue underneath, orange-hued above. Look out at the garden, tell me about the heat the way one talks of a catastrophe!

Do you think the chestnut-tree is going to die? It holds up its frizzled leaves to the sky, the colour of mottled marble. . . . And nothing can save the roses, caught in the flame before they've opened. . . . Roses . . . dewy roses, swollen with the night rain, chill to the touch. . . .

Oh, come away from the window! Deceive my languor with tales of flowers bowed under the rain! Deceive yourself, tell me of the storm yonder, with bulging violet back, of the rising wind that rears up against the house, rustling the vine and the wistaria, tell of the first heavy drops slanting in through the open window! I'll drink them from my hands, taste in them the dust of distant roads, the pall of low cloud that bursts over the town. . . .

Do you recall the last storm, the bitter water that weighed down the beautiful marigolds, the sugared rain dripping from the honey-suckle, the silver-spangled fronded fennel from which we sucked a flavour of fine absinthe in a thousand droplets! . . .

More, more, I'm so hot! Remind me of the quicksilver that quivers in the hollow of the nasturtiums after a shower and on the downy mint. . . . Picture the dew, the high breeze that bows the tree-tops but doesn't brush my hair. . . . Picture the pond, surrounded by mosquitoes and dancing tree-frogs. . . . Oh, how I'd like to hold the cool belly of a little frog in either hand! . . . I'm hot, if you only knew it. . . . Go on talking. . . .

Go on talking, cure my fever! Evoke autumn for me, give me, prematurely, the chill grape that's picked at dawn, and the last strawberries of October, ripe on one side only. . . . Yes, I'd like to crush in my dry hands a bunch of grapes forgotten on the vine,

a little wrinkled by the frost. . . . Couldn't you call up two fine
dogs with very cold noses? You see, I'm really ill, I'm wandering.

Don't leave me! Sit down and read me the story that begins:
'The princess was born in a country where the snow always covers
the ground, and her palace was made of ice and frost. . . .' Of frost,
d'you hear, of frost! . . . When I repeat that sparkling word, I
feel that I'm biting into a ball of crunchy snow, a fine winter-
apple made by my own hands. . . . Ah, I'm hot! . . . I'm hot,
but . . . something stirs in the air. . . . Is it only that golden wasp?
Does it herald the end of this long day? I abandon myself to you.
Call down on me clouds, evening, sleep. Your fingers at the nape
of my neck untangle the damp disorder of my hair. . . . Bend over
me, fan my nostrils with your breath, squeeze over my teeth the
sour juice of the currant you're biting. . . .

I've almost stopped grumbling, though you wouldn't know if
it's because I'm relaxed. . . . Don't go away if I fall asleep; I'll
pretend not to know when you kiss my wrists and arms, cooler
now, beaded like the necks of the brown water-coolers. . . .

Respite

'Did they tell you that while you were away I led a lonely exis-
tence, unsociable and faithful, apparently waiting impatiently? . . .
Don't believe it. I'm neither lonely nor faithful. And it's not you
I'm waiting for.

'Don't get upset! Read this letter right through to the end. I
enjoy taunting you when you're far away, when you can't do
anything to me, only clench your fists and break a vase. . . . I
enjoy taunting you without any risk, seeing you—separated by
distance—quite small, angry and harmless. . . . You're the watch-
dog and I'm the cat in the tree. . . .

'I'm not waiting for you. Did they say that I threw open my

window at sunrise, longing for the day when you'd stride down
the path, chasing your long shadow before you up to my
balcony? They were lying. If I have left my bed, pale and still
dazed by sleep, it's not the sound of your step that beckoned
me. . . . How beautiful it is, the light, empty avenue! My gaze
encounters no obstruction from dead branch or straw, and the
blue stripe of your shadow no longer moves over the clear sand,
patterned only by the birds' small claws.

'I was only awaiting . . . that moment, the start of the day, my
own, the one I share with no one. I let you take hold there just
long enough to welcome you, to seize your coolness, the dew of
your path across the meadows, and close the shutters on us. . . .
Now the dawn is mine alone, and I alone enjoy it, rosy and be-
dewed, like an untouched fruit despised by others. It's for that I
abandon my sleep, and my dream that's now and then of you. . . .
You see. Barely awake, I leave you in order to betray you. . . .

'Did they also tell you that around noon I went down, barefooted, to the sea? They were watching, weren't they? They've
praised me to you for my sullen solitude and the still, aimless pro-
cession of my footsteps on the beach; they've pitied my bowed
face, suddenly watchful, turned towards . . . towards what?
Towards whom? Oh! If you could have only heard! I was
laughing, laughing as you've never heard me laugh! It's because
there, on the wave-smoothed beach, there's no longer the slightest
trace of your games, your gambolling, your youthful violence,
your cries no longer sound in the wind, and your swimmer's
prowess no longer shatters the harmonious curve of the wave that
rises, bends, rolls up like a transparent green leaf, and breaks at
my feet. . . .

'Waiting for you, looking for you? Not here, where nothing
remembers you. The sea rocks no boat, the gull that was fishing,
clasping a wave and flapping its wings, has flown away. The
reddish, lion-shaped rock stretches, violet, under the water attack-
ing it. Is it possible that you once spurned that lion under your
bare heel? The sand that crackles as it dries, like heated silk, did
you ever trample it, forage in it, did it soak up odour and sea-salt
from you? I say all this to myself as I walk on the beach at noon
and shake my head incredulously. But sometimes I turn round

and look about me like children who frighten themselves with
made-up stories—no, no, you're not there—I've been afraid. I
suddenly thought I might find you there, looking as if you wanted
to steal my thoughts . . . I was afraid.

'There's nothing—only the smooth beach that crackles as if
under an invisible flame, only splinters of shells that pierce the
sand, fly up to prick one's nose, fall down again and hem the
seashore with a thousand broken, glinting stitches. . . . It's only
midday. I haven't finished with you, absent one! I run towards
the shadowy room where the blue daylight is reflected in the
polished table, in the brown paunch of the sideboard; its coolness
smells of the wine-cellar and the fruit store-room, thanks to the
cider that froths in the jug and a handful of cherries in the fold of
a cabbage-leaf. . . .

'Only one place is laid. The other side of the table, opposite me,
glimmers like a pool. You know, I shan't put the rose there that
you used to find every morning, limp on your plate. I'll pin it to
my blouse, high up near the shoulder, so that I need only turn my
head slightly to brush it with my lips. . . . How big the window is!
You used to half-screen it from me and I never saw, till now,
the mauve, almost white, underside of the drooping clematis
flowers. . . .

'I hum quite quietly, quite quietly, just to myself. . . . The
biggest strawberry, the blackest cherry, it's not in your mouth but
in mine that they melt so deliciously. . . . You used to covet them
so much that I gave them to you, not out of tenderness, but from
a sort of shocked good manners. . . .

'The whole afternoon lies before me like a sloping terrace, all
radiant above and plunging down below into the indistinct, lake-
coloured evening. It's the time—perhaps they've told you—when
I seclude myself. Faithful seclusion, eh? The sad, voluptuous
meditation of a solitary sweetheart?. . . What do you know about
it? Can you know the names I give the illusions I cherish, my
thronging advisers, can you be sure that my dream bears your
features?. . . Don't trust me! Don't trust me, you who've caught
me unawares, crying and laughing, you whom I betray every
moment, you whom I kiss saying, very softly, "Stranger". . . .

'Until the evening I betray you. But when it's night I'll rendezvous with you and the full moon will find me beneath the tree where the nightingale was so frenzied, so drunk from singing, that he did not hear our footfalls or our sighs or our mingled words. . . . No single day of mine is like the day before, but a night of full moon is divinely like any other night of full moon. . . .

'Does your spirit fly through space, across sea and mountain, to the rendezvous I've made with you, under the tree? I'll be there as I've promised, unsteady as my head, thrown back, seeks vainly for the arm that once supported it. . . . I call you—because I know you won't come. Behind my closed eyelids I conjure with your image, soften the colour of your glance, the sound of your voice, I shape your hair to my liking, refine your mouth, and I refashion you—discerning, playful, indulgent, tender—I change you, correct you. . . .

'I change you . . . gradually and completely, even to the name you bear. . . . And then I depart, furtive and embarrassed, on tiptoe, as if, having joined you under the tree's shadow, I left with a stranger. . . .'

Invalid

As on every morning a slender lilac wand, an erect pillar of light, cleaves the darkness of the room. It stands out sharply against the ornate, sombre background of my dream, a dream of gardens with dense verdure, foliage as blue as that in tapestries, gardens that murmur languidly under a warm breeze. . . . I close my eyes again, in the hope of reconciling, beyond the luminous shaft, the two sumptuous panels of my dream. A pain, centred exactly at my eyebrows, brings me quite awake. But the stormy rustling of the blue foliage lingers in my ears.

I reach for the lamp, which blossoms from the shadow like a rosy gourd, trailing behind it the dry tendrils of silken threads. . . .

The painful throbbing persists behind my eyebrows. I swallow painfully; something like a rough arbutus berry sticks in my throat, I clench my fists and hide my nails to avoid the touch of the sheets.

Cold, hot—shivering. . . . Ill? Yes. Decidedly yes. Not very ill— just enough. I put out the light and the luminous shaft, an icy blue that cools my fever, reappears between the curtains. It's six o'clock.

Ill. . . . Oh yes, ill at last! A little influenza, perhaps? I shut my eyes once more and wait for the day to begin as if it were my birthday. A whole long day of weakness, semi-sleep, of humoured cravings and pampered feeding! As it is, I want the fragrance of lemon-flavoured eau-de-Cologne around my bed—and when I'm hungry there will also be the odours of warm vanillaed milk and roast apples frosted with sugar. . . .

Must I wait for the household to wake up? Or shall I ring to make them hurry, startled, with slippers slapping on the stairs, with exclamations of 'My God!' and 'It was only to be expected, there's flu about. . . .' Better to wait, spying the growing daylight, the carpet that pales and brightens like a pool. . . . Vaguely I hear vehicles passing, the tinkling of the bottles hanging from the milkman's fingers. . . . The diapason of a bass drum sounded gently and regularly, muffles my ears and shuts out the noises of the street; it's the monotonous, pleasant ground swell of my fever. Far from trying to forget it, I encourage it, I study it, I fit into its rhythm the simple tunes and songs of my childhood. . . . Ah, now, borne on music towards the gardens abandoned by my dreams, I glimpse again that dense blue foliage. . . .

'. . . What? What d'you want? I'm sleeping. . . . Yes, you can see I'm ill. Yes, yes, really ill! No, I don't want anything, except for you not to burst suddenly into my room. . . . And don't touch the curtains—oh, how insensitive well people are! Have you done with opening and closing them, waving great flags of light that chill the whole room?

'Just give me . . . a glass of iced water. I want just a plain glass, a goblet free of flaw or ornament, thin, grateful to the lips and tongue, filled with sparkling water that seems a little blue because of the silver dish—I'm thirsty. . . .

'No? You refuse? Ah, burning with fever, what do I want with your infusion smelling of boiled linen and dead flowers? Clear out, all of you! I loathe you! No one's to hug me with their cold noses, no one's to touch me with the blunt chapped hands of an early-risen governess. . . .

'Go away! I'll enjoy the perverse frail pleasure of being ill more when I'm by myself. I feel so superior to you all today! Sensitive sore eyes, longing for soft lights and muted reflections—delicate ears, moving under my hair, disturbed by any sound—a skin capable of detecting any flaw in the linen clothing it—and a miraculous sense of smell that evokes at will, in this room, the scent of orange-flowers or bruised bananas, or the overripe muskmelon that splits to spread its blood-stained juice.

'I feel that there, behind the door, you must be a little jealous, you who can't conjure, as I do, with the November sun that falls gently on the roof down there, at the bottom of the garden, with the branch bent by each breeze, each time dipping the tips of its mildewed leaves in a bright ray. . . . It springs back and now it's pink. . . . Violet, pink . . . pink, violet . . . violet-blue, like the foliage of my dream . . . they're not so far away, those blue leaves, their marine murmur fills my ears; shall I have time enough to dwell in their shade?

'. . . Who's there? What's the matter? I was asleep. . . . Why do you leave me alone? How long have you left me here, too weak to call out? Come here, help me. . . . Oh! You don't care for me a bit. . . . But who left this bunch of violets by my face while I was asleep? Give them here, so I can touch them. . . . How fresh and cool and grateful on the lips! . . . Yes, I know, the pavement was dry and blue, my dogs ran in front of you in the path in the Bois, they stirred up a squall of leaves . . . I'm jealous. . . . Don't look at me; I wish I were small enough to cry unashamedly. I don't want to be ill any more. I'll be good; I'll drink the bitter draught, the infusion too. Isn't it yet time to light the lamp? Don't bother to lie, I shall hear well enough when the children run shouting out of school, and the clogs of the bread-woman who comes at five o'clock. . . .

'Tell me, would you stay with me so faithfully, indulgent and scolding, if I were ill for a long, long time? Or if I suddenly grew old, imprisoned as old people are? It makes one shudder to think of it. . . . It makes one shudder. . . . Why do you think it's fever that makes me shudder? I shudder because it's the evil hour, the twilight hour*. . . . Quick! Light the lamp so that its glow scares off the phantom dog, the ghostly wolf. . . .

'See, I don't shiver any more now that it's shining, enormous, round and pink like a colocynth with ornate skin. . . . What a beautiful fruit, and from what a fabulous garden! It still clings to its torn-off tendrils, trailing over the table, and perhaps, if I close my eyes. . . . Wait, yes, I can see the branch that bears the fruit and the tree beyond the branch, the blue tree, at last, at last! And all that dark garden, beaten down by the hot wind, rustling with water and leaves, the dream-garden I shall always thirst for, after tonight. . . .'

* *L'heure entre chien et loup.*

Four Seasons

Christmas Presents

More productive of worry than gratification, these two words shine like a shimmering frost-flower over a dark doorway that's about to open. Let's face it, we who give but no longer receive, we parents and old friends, are in the grip of an annual anxiety. And with good reason. The least demanding of our wards, the youngest of our children, may confine their requests to a bicycle! Ours is a terrible era. The lisping babe covets a cine-camera. 'You know, I'm still waiting for my five horsepower,' confides the first communicant. 'What do you want for your New Year gift?' a godfather asked his eight-year-old godchild. She turned towards him the frank blue eyes that seemed just to be discovering the world and answered simply : 'A bedroom, mine's worn out.'

I know of parents who sigh with discomfiture when their offspring demand a fur-coat at the age of ten, a car at twelve, and a string of small pearls at fifteen. They cross-examine each other in detail to discover the causes of this precocious maturity that resembles a perversion. 'In our day. . . .'

I nod my head out of politeness. But I know nothing of 'their' day, nor they of mine. I know that, for me, 'New Year's Day' was not taken to mean presents, excursions, shops, insincere good wishes and empty pockets. . . .

Empty they virtually were, the hands and pockets of those who showered me, nevertheless, with favours and every kind of gift. But they achieved miracles within their means. Before daybreak, a red streak across the snow, on 1st January, the hundred pounds of bread, baked for the poor, were already warming the tiled kitchen of the house where I was born, and the hundred ten-centime pieces clinked in a basket. A pound of bread, a ten-centime piece, and the poor folk of yesteryear went on their way, grateful and unpretentious, calling me by my childhood nickname. Standing gravely upright in my sabots, I distributed the hewn bread, the big pennies; on my hands I could smell the appetizing odour of the fresh loaves; and surreptitiously I licked the wheat-flour from beneath the braided belly of a twelve-pound loaf. In my recollections the smell of new bread is closely linked with the sound of cock-crow beneath the red streak of dawn in the depths of winter and the drumstick variations of the towncrier on my father's doorstep. How keenly I still feel it in my heart, this memory of an icy holiday with no gifts other than a few sweets, some silver-wrapped tangerines, a book. . . . The night before, the traditional cake sauced with a flaming sauce of rum and apricot, served around ten o'clock, and a cup of pale, fragrant China tea had ushered in the evening's vigil. A crackling, leaping fire, a few books, the sighs of sleeping dogs, sparse words—whence did the hearts of me and mine derive their joy? And how transmit that sober happiness, that darkly glowing happiness, to our children of today? Who has made them so grasping and sophisticated? Modern life, this harsh era, and we ourselves. . . . Ourselves, because our guilt dates from that first neglect, the first shame that followed and declared within us: 'Just when your child most needed your presence, your advice, your understanding help, you compensated for your failure with a gift, when what was needed was yourself. . . . And then you did it all over again. . . .'

It's the fashion to feel a cheap superiority over the younger generations, to shake one's head and declare: 'When we were the age of these children we were content with trifles, always the same cake, always the same little tree, a simple statement of sentiments and good wishes, always the same. . . .'

Ah yes, always the same. Who changed it for us? From sentiment and economy of effort, the child fears anything that may disturb an exact recollection, a picture whose every detail is fondly preserved by his implacable memory. Did I not seek with an expert tongue in the annual cake, speckled with raisins, the exact flavour of the previous year's cake? Did I not summon to aid my gustatory faculties the unchanging colours of carpet and lampshade, the howling of the east wind under the door, the smell of a fine new book, the grain of its binding a little sticky?

The joy of the five senses! On these delights, that might be called pagan, a domestic religion is founded, and the spirit warms itself at the smallest flame, if the small flame endures. Parents, around your faces—which don't age for them—arrange at Christmas for your still tottering children a setting that time will barely alter. No matter if it lacks ostentation. For the lights of the feast will become ritual, and the flowers or the holly, and also—a little —those words that will evoke Christmas during the rest of the year or the midnight vigil of New Year's Eve. It's only the old who find the invisible, irrevocable passage of time so poignant. A child's emotion, when one re-creates for him a picture from his brief past, does not depend on surprise or wonder. He cherishes what he already knows, prefers what he knows, and chants it within himself to the rhythm of a spontaneous poetry.

Enough, I'd say, of careful diplomacy and circumspect approach to surprise those of our little ones who display the current mode—bored, contemptuous of simple offerings. It's hopeless to try to please them by stuffing them. An effort at restraint, a return to a more refined conception of the annual holidays, is a noble exercise. And we penitent instructors should not overlook the fact that such a sentimental exercise, like every exercise, trains instructor as much as pupil.

Visits

Visits, terror of my childhood, uneasy burden of my life as a young woman! Wedding visits, postprandial visits, visits of condolence and congratulation, New Year's Day visits especially! . . . Do the number of hours I've devoted to you surpass the forty-day lifespan of a long-lived butterfly? I think not. I can't believe that such a brief purgatory could compensate for all my sins.

In children the desire and the need for sociability should be fostered. Where could I have acquired this need, this desire? A happy childhood is a bad preparation for human contacts, and mine was fully engaged with fond relatives, somewhat eccentric, rich in personality and a grim sensibility. The shrill bell at the

threshold of the house where I was born used to herald the inva-
sion—the Visit!—and dispersed even the cats. My brothers scattered like Chouans,* intimately acquainted with the escape-route
and its rustic hiding-places, and I followed them. My mother
would shout 'Little savages!', spying in us, with secret approba-
tion, her own inborn wildness. . . . She never realized that the
jungle no longer exists for the children of men and that—before
pleasure, across all grief, above private dramas and work—there
looms the rite, religion and duty of the Visit. I learned this late.
I learned it at an age when there no longer burned within me any
regimented faith. How could it endure, my patience in visiting
two Aunt Marys, several aged relatives named Henrietta, and
those families, allied and alike to one another, who dragged me
here and there beset with a kind of feeble vertigo produced by
fear, fatigue and an empty stomach?

New Year's Day in Paris is not often blessed with good weather.
The rain mixed with snow, a thaw more penetrating than the
frost, a sudden shower of fine snowflakes soon glazed with thin
ice, all added to the mournfulness of the holiday. And as a very
young newly-wed I dared not break with the conventions of
in-laws whose combined kindliness and high moral tone seemed
to my youthful vigour and zest for life like a strait-jacket that
incites to suicide. The whole deadly day I proceeded from visit to
visit with the anguished soul of a prisoner. Along a path blazed
by dry cakes, cups of tea and black-clothed women, I encountered
seasoned sisters-in-law, cousins scattered over Paris from the
Passage des Eaux to the Grand-Montrouge, nieces studded with
chilblains, and uncles by marriage—elderly brothers, invariably
confused by me when one of them died. . . . I also encountered
civilized dejected children, used to the unprotesting sacrifice of
their free day, their afternoon's devouring reading, stoic children
who would give up their seat in a bus or their place in Paradise
with the same stiff, submissive expression. I wasn't taken in by
their passivity. A schoolboy who is unhappy or teased at school
bequeaths to the man he becomes his scholastic phobias, the re-
gressive dreams that wake him at night, that most tragic of

* Rebel Breton Royalists of 1793.

examinees' dreams—the nightmare imposition. Even at that time, twenty years ago, I should have liked to apply to those ill-employed adolescents the wise counsel of a marquise to her grandson : 'Make only those mistakes that you really enjoy'; I should have liked to say to them : 'Perform only those duties that are meaningful. In so doing find the desire and firm intention to visit your friends when mutual affection impels you. There's no grace or sincerity about today. There's not even a holly-sprig or mistletoe-berry, pagan ornaments of Christmas, or the spirit-sprinkled yule log. . . . It's devoid of everything, even the sharp lasting cold, fleecy with snow, the cold—if I may so describe it—that keeps one warm and excites laughter, sliding and sport, the heavy white backcloth that enhances the yellow of the orange, the pink of children's cheeks and satin handbags, that makes the beggar's coarse, extended, mittened hand more welcome. Your greeting, spiteful and embarrassed, no longer moves from door to door with a gay clatter of clogs; it lies in ambush, waiting to be paid its toll. . . . The truth is, my poor children, it's a miserable day that stinks of cash and has lost its good odour of friendship. . . .'

Those children of yesteryear never heard what I preached *in petto*. Today my twelve-year-old daughter radiates an untrammelled worldly sociability, and she it is who informs me that human beings are never so stubborn as when it comes to imagined duty. But, in fact, I know how much the determination of reformers is worth when the reforms they advocate stigmatize the puerility of our manners and customs. I've known this ever since a cousin of mine left a visiting-card bearing the engraved words :

RAPHAEL LANDOY

Vice-President of the League against the Use of Visiting-Cards

Tomorrow's Springtime

In January the saffron rose climbs the uprights of the Monégasque pergolas, assaults the Nice palm-tree, lifts itself to the light, turns its face to the sun and unfolds, in an instant, a corolla of incomparable amber flesh colour and perfumed disorder. . . . 'There you are,' says this hardy harbinger. 'That's the pink Paris will be wearing . . . four months from now !'

From December on the first white dresses, blossoming beside the green lawns of the Riviera, display a certain arrogance. 'Look at this waist, as long as a rainy day, this embryonic panel that's an excuse for a skirt, this tube of material minus any curve or belt, this brimless hat that protects neither the complexion nor the eyes —that's what Paris will go crazy over when the spring comes. We may be white, here. But Paris will see us multicoloured. We are like the "mock-ups" that the model-makers and costume designers of the great Revues deliver "in blank"—and no mistake—to the whims of the colourists. But the whole springtide of fashion is already within us. White as a sleeping virgin, we await only the earth's awakening to assume the colours of the bud, the yellow daisy, the blue gentian and the flushed wild rose.'

I watch them pass, these white cocoons of linen, supple silk, spotless wool and simple cashmere, and I sigh. A new fashion year is about to begin, fatal again for those women whom Nature has provided with unambiguous contours. It's true that the species is becoming rare. But it has a hard time of it—as I know only too well. Alas, I could never—as did a fashionable woman in a restaurant who had stained her snowy dress with a drop of gravy —run to the washroom and return triumphant and immaculate —at least in front, for she had simply turned her dress back to front. . . .

Yes, spring pronounces that the fashion will be flat and short. A spring for women to stand poised like a slim lamp-post at the angle of a building, to start up from a lawn like a fountain, to lean against a balustrade like a pillar less bulging than the others.

Walking, golf and tennis—you will be more in vogue than ever; we shall see our Dianas always fleet and never seated, and for good reason. For, if they should sit down, their short, tight, sweet, miserable little skirts will ride up beyond what is permissible, exposing stockings to which inflexible whim has given the exact shade of the dolls we used to make out of bran. Let them sit down —and behold them, I won't say embarrassed, but sometimes embarrassing. However, most of them are devoid of ulterior motive, used to their partial nudity, as untroubled as our half-naked children, and they lower neither the hem of their skirts nor their eyelashes. Once a woman would show her leg because the leg was pretty—she might conceal it for similar reasons. Today the leg is a neutral prolongation and completion of the shape of the garment; beneath twelve inches of visible skirt the *couturier* demands twelve inches of visible leg, no more, no less; he doesn't ask you women for your opinion and it doesn't matter much if these last twelve inches are sticks, spindles or pillars, or if they are mounted on boats, does' feet, or dull slices of bread and butter.

Short, flat, geometric, rectangular, the female garment is based on patterns that derive from parallelograms, and 1925 is not going to witness the return of the fashion for flowing curves, jutting breasts and lascivious hips. An adventurous designer has imported into France half a dozen American mannequins who are surely not going to settle matters for you, you sturdy French ponies, strapping Latins inured to fatigue, resistant to disease. This squad of archangels, in a chaste flight unimpeded by the flesh, will reorientate fashion towards an increasingly slender line, clothes increasingly simplified in the making, cut with a single scissorslash from magnificent material.

The time can't be far off when the *haute couture*, having created a kind of luxurious indigence, will be dismayed by its work. It favours anyone capable of cutting out from two lengths of material a double rectangle pierced by two sleeves, on which the embroiderer, the weaver, not to mention the colourist, will subsequently exert themselves. Whenever *couture* has created a design so strict, so like a uniform that only colour, ornament and consistency can add distinguishing features, it has rashly abandoned an important part of its prerogatives. A certain excess of refinement, proceeding by elimination, exposes the creation to a danger that the properly jealous designer must always dread—facility.

Farewell to the Snow

The first curtain of cypress erect against the rising sun, the first Mediterranean bay buried like an axe-head between two hillsides, the first orange-tree and the first rose—in the train that brought us from Paris the evening before we concede them the easy conquest of our heart. But the winter sun now has a rival—the clean enduring snow, bluely reflecting the circumambient azure.

I haven't been acquainted with it very long. I still don't know how to make use of it as well as the multicoloured children, gliding on their winged feet or upright on the firm but yielding sledge, who play on its flanks and traverse its violet crevasses. I could gauge its power from the first gulps of air that carried a glacial taste of peppermint to the very depths of my lungs. The snow a country? The snow a climate? No, a planet. There the conqueror's lust is stayed in dream. Only on the snow nowadays can the races meet in full sociability. Its tranquil chaos welcomes the stranger, who can abandon there his spleen, his chauvinism, his advancing years. For it conceals the earth, that earth whose living texture a man cannot touch, whose odour he cannot breathe, without again becoming a savage and temperamental pioneer.

Only on the snow can both sexagenarian and child squat on the same small sledges and abandon themselves to the slopes. They feel alike and exchange smiles. They don't envy the bobsleigh, that clamorous meteor that skims devouring the air between its double spray of pulverized ice. Space and giddy incline are the realm of the toboggan also. Its drivers handle two reins which the little runnered sledge can well dispense with. But before every driver of an enchanted sledge there marches a phantom charger, and the two ends of the sledge-rope most certainly girdle the neck and bridle the mouth of a mare of transparent frost speeding at thirty miles an hour. My faëry-mare knew perfectly well that she was pulling a passenger addicted to worldly pleasures. She slewed round to a halt that deposited me on the very threshold of a chalet where red herrings were curing in pine-smoke, where cheese, mixed with alcohol and boiling wine, wept heavy, succulent tears on the toast. A pale insidious white wine conveyed to my palate the very temperature of the ice-pail where the glass jug nestled; and the domestic poetry and lyricism engendered by appetite steamed from the sizzling stewpot and in the blue breaths of us well-fed mountaineers.

O simple, precarious, eternal realm of snow! You turn a man into a gay child, intent and devoted to his playful leisure. You have created this indulgence—the duty to amuse oneself, the right to live in a body which, from every hour devoted to you, enhances in perfection, pulsing with new strength at every fall. You see your disciples leaving their hotel at morning twilight, the time when the speeding dawn leaves the foot of the mountain slumbering in violet shadow but carves on its face an orange hue of heavy, incandescent metal slashing across the blue. They depart, with their long, tapering wooden blades across one shoulder, their double stick in hand. They are as grave and quiet as if they were all ten years old.

The previous day they'd chosen today's objective, some arbitrary invisible point—a mountain peak or perhaps a chalet hidden under its snow-furred porch. Here or there, what matter? Here or there, so long as it's at the cost of rhythmic exertion, mental and physical exercise, so long as they reach a peak of mental and physical exaltation, so long as, standing somewhere very high against the dark blue that burdens the peaks, constrained to open arms and heart to embrace their Eden, they attain an inexpressible happiness. They return at noon, steaming with joy and healthy sweat, their small, deep-blue shadow crouching at their feet. Or perhaps they do not return till evening, laggard and silent, and their silence seems full of poetry because they are beyond thought. O snow, they are your satiated lovers! They have possessed you alone since daybreak, and you have satisfied them. They have seen the mountain diminish under their tread, the scenery expand. Halted, they sat on a fold of your virginal garment, turning from side to side as the sun burned their shoulders. Hollow and light-headed with hunger, they rummaged in their pockets and ate facing the sun, careful to gather the scraps. Then they bound their blades to their feet and began their flights above the little valleys. As they leaped they saw the concave expanse fall away, return, to be distanced once again. . . . Their falls powdered them with snow; they plunged head-first into the spangled craters where the sun cast the seven colours of the rainbow.

They have rivalled each other in audacity and speed. They have not pursued or slaughtered harmless game. They gave no thought to the love of women or their neighbour's good. For you require your devotees to be chaste, O snow, and you purify them. At night they sleep the long sleep of children and are faithful to you even in dreams. They behold you in their dreams and fly even better than the day before. Your silence enters unimpeded through their big open window and nothing stirs in your realm, which the wind cannot reach, except the pulsating gleam of the stars. They sleep, forgetting for a few hours the dedication they owe you, and it's you, greedy for their company, who sometimes descends in showers, moves hesitating about their slumber, and empties on their bedspread a melting tribute of snowflakes, immaculate jewels that dissolve like the content of a dream at the first hint of day.

Models

Two men, five men, ten, twenty . . . I stopped counting them. They attend this ritual of *couture* more eagerly than any boule-vard parade. They profess to 'adore' these processions of dresses and pretty girls, of materials whose ever-diminishing coverage calls for ever-increasing magnificence. They loudly proclaim their liking for those vestimentary rites that every recognized designer organizes with theatrical or religious pomp. Monsieur accompanies Madame to these shows and Madame tilts her chin as if to imply: 'Yes, yes, it's just that he wants a close look at the models!' In which she's often wrong. For Monsieur is capable of one or two pure sentiments, among them the appreciation of colour, movement, form and, especially, novelty. Men at the *couturier's* have long discarded the embarrassment of big boys caught playing marbles, the awkwardness of castaways thrown up by storm on the Isle of Women. Only men derive a total pleasure, unmarred by covetousness, from the parade of models. While his companion, secretly frantic, broken-heartedly renounces a little 'creation' at six thousand francs, the man beams, observes, takes note of X's low waistline and Z's draperies as he might absorb the characteristics of a school of painting. He can appreciate an *ensemble* better than a woman. He can assess the model quite objectively, better than the woman. While the female spectator is feverishly murmuring to herself 'I'd like that one, and that one, and that dress there', the male quietly admires the copper hair and milky pallor of the red-headed model, set in a bronze sheath more revealing than any swimsuit. He realizes that the absinthe- and moonlight-coloured tunic could not be separated, without losing its value, from the young blonde with a greyhound's dignity of carriage, coiffed with long hair unblemished by steel or scissors. He knows what a grave responsibility rests on the girl his wife calls 'that creature' between her teeth; and he would be distressed if anyone who desired the dress wanted to take it away as the designer conceived it, across the shoulders of the dazzling young woman whose voice he hasn't even heard.

In short, a man now feels at home wherever feminine adornment is arranged and displayed, and current snobbishness finds him at his ease there; for there, as the models parade, he can meet the artist fashion favours, the woman of the world and her novelist, the parliamentarian and his Egeria. The model glides from one group to the next, a long gleaming shuttle weaving her web. The model, a disturbing colleague, is the end-point of a concerted effort that everyone now recognizes. The public appreciates

the part played by the weaver, the designer, the cutter, the saleswoman, the *couturier* who directs them all; but, as far as the
model is concerned, it is more reserved, it ponders—admiring or
suspicious. Among all the modernized aspects of the most luxurious
of industries, the model, a vestige of voluptuous barbarianism, is
like some plunder-laden prey. She is the object of unbridled
regard, a living bait, the passive realization of an ideal. Her
ambiguous profession makes her ambiguous. Even her sex is ver-
bally uncertain. People say : 'This model is charming';* and her
job is to excite covetousness, a demoralizing mission that distances
her from both *patron* and ordinary workers. Isn't that enough to
justify and excuse the model's strange capriciousness? No other
female occupation contains such potent impulses to moral dis-
integration as this one, applying as it does the outward signs of
riches to a poor and beautiful girl.

'Patience,' you say, 'everything will change; the advancement
of the model is in train. We designers, we'll turn the model into
a loyal colleague, properly and punctually salaried, able to live
decently on her grace and beauty. . . .'

Gentlemen designers, I'd like to believe you. But if I'm not
mistaken, you're hardly there yet. Granted, you pay up to forty
thousand francs a year for the quivering shoulder, the noble neck,
the regal carriage of those who, more than any other female
creatures, exalt the products of your genius. All right. You claim
to give your model not only an adequate honorarium but the
esteem and trust you bestow, for instance, on your leading sales-
lady. You don't want to see your slim, elegant Diana swooning
and yawning in your salon after who knows what nocturnal esca-
pades. There speaks an honest man with an understanding heart.
But beauty is one thing and bureaucracy another. Beauty is meant
for admiration, and you fit her out to increase this admiration. On
matters of love and war you say to Beauty : 'This is your domain,
you're not to go any farther. Use this salon, this gallery, for your
deer-park. Walk, come back, turn round, come back again.
Though half-naked, you're not to admit to feeling cold until the
time when, leaving your audience, you find yourself alone and

---

* I.e. *ce mannequin.*

shivering. You must understand that this year we want you rid of all superfluous flesh, as tough as any gymnast. But you're not to indulge in any sport, so eat as little as possible and don't spoil yourself buying roast chestnuts at the street-corner. . . .'

Visionaries! Do you really want your arrogantly beautiful models, imprisoned in your luxury, awash with coffee, deprived of the manual work that steadies the heartbeat and regulates thought, to acquire the souls of accountants? But that's not the end of your problems, though your effort is a praiseworthy one. You may recruit and guard your wayward model, hoping for ultimate success, hoping that the lure of gain and a liking for tranquil independence will provide you with beautiful young women of unruffled countenance and placid temperament.

Nevertheless, you will induce in her over an undetermined period the neurasthenia, the nervous yawning, the tearful outbursts and unforeseen fatigue, the brief acclaim singling her out for tribute, the graceful trampling underfoot, like natal soil, of matchless luxury—you will foster all this in her that you tolerate, that you excuse, that you respect, in her favoured brother—the artist.

Elegance, Economy

Was it the same one? Or perhaps another, and another, and yet another? 'Not quite the same nor yet quite different. . . .' I'm referring to the young woman in black satin and pink stockings who contravened both hygiene and commonsense this winter, you know the lady I mean. . . .

February and March have poured on Paris the blackest rain that ever fell from a grey sky, snow the colder because it melts, hail crackling underfoot like a broken necklace. In March, on some miserable afternoons, you can see the drayhorses halt with lowered heads under the half-liquid, half-frozen downpours, taxi-drivers run for the nearest bar, delivery boys under open porches turn into statues of polished oilskin. You can see the hesitant bus, the blinded, pondering tram. You can see the place de l'Opéra, the boulevard and the rue de la Paix deserted, gleaming, bombarded by the wrath from on high. . . .

It was in this weather, in such times of meteorological disturbance, that I saw her, the woman in a marocain or black satin coat, shod with three small patent-leather straps, legs clad in silk the hue of urticaria or a bilious attack. Swathed in badger, but with feet nearly bare, she went her hardened way, chin jutting, stomach out, and backside tucked in.

She encountered—too rarely—her antagonist, the woman in a black macintosh, a waterproof raincoat or fisherman's sou'wester. The latter strode along, sturdy on stout soles, feet warm in ribbed woollen stockings. One day I recognized my friend Valentine, sheltering and shivering beneath the Roman archway of a *porte cochère*. She was paddling in the general quagmire, waiting for it to clear up. I accosted her to tell her off, to call her to account for her unsuitable get-up. She replied, with the acerbity attendant on an incipient laryngitis: 'My dear, do you really think, with material and fashions costing what they do, that I can afford thirty-six outfits to suit every change of weather?'

For women have retained several military expressions from the war, they say 'outfit' where they used to say 'costume'. My friend Valentine was content with the figure thirty-six. Less definite, more exaggerated than a hundred thousand, she brandished it under my nose like a shield with her miserable little conical umbrella, this thirty-six. But I wanted to conduct a serious inquiry and I insisted on knowing whether, in a feminine budget, economy need banish elegance, that supreme elegance that consists of wearing the right garment at the right time, in the right place and circumstances. My friend Valentine's shudder, like a chicken under a downpour, showed that I'd put my finger on the spot where indiscretion ends and sacrilege begins. One may always tease a woman, even unkindly, about her short matt hair, her scraggy schoolgirl neck, her shoulder-blades like those of a starved chicken, her too-short dress, her slop-pail hat, her Kanaka jewellery. But one can only venture with extreme caution, using rubber gloves and a miner's lamp, into the domain where a woman, constrained to use her own initiative, has chosen badly instead of well.

Pressed on another occasion to explain why she had opted all winter for an all-purpose outfit of a coat-dress of black satin with a collar and facings of lynx, superimposed—dare I add—on dish-rag stockings and sieves of shoes, my friend Valentine ungraciously admitted : 'You see, this not only saves me the expense of a woollen costume, the silk coat over a satin or georgette dress make a "number" that can cope with any daily emergency, lunch out, even dinner, dancing or a theatre. . . . Why, only the other day. . . .'

I didn't hear much of what followed. I was clinging to a truth, a feminine truth, somewhat condensed and cloudy, but a truth nonetheless. 'That can cope with any emergency. . . .' Since the first rape, Woman, afraid of nothing, has not forgotten to watch out for emergencies. And yet she is lazy, and laziness often distracts her from a healthily vigilant coquetry. You think her changeable, diverse? Hardly, for what is her dream? To be dressed and got up, as she says, 'once and for all'. When she had her hair cut short she thought she'd wake up in the morning with her hair done once and for all. But the coiffeur, lord of the curls, pruner of the neck, with the copyright of a certain twist of hair by the ear, was alert; and I know many a freed woman who already groans : 'Oh, it's too much . . . I shall have to get it cut every fortnight . . . and that curl behind my ear won't stay put. . . .'

Decked and groomed at ten o'clock like prize horses, how many women approach their second *toilette* before dinner with any eagerness? How many of you are nonchalantly content with a 'paint-job' performed in a restaurant cloakroom? Powder and rouge in clouds, a stroke of the comb, a brushing of hands and nails. . . . And then one undoes the coat-dress that still shows— but let's not inspect it too closely—a few splashes of sandy mud from the Bois to reveal a flat, gold-spangled tunic, embroidered in a hundred colours, and one feels ready for a good night out.

It's you I meet so often in the mornings, by the lakes, you apostles of economic elegance. You walk quickly, noses buried in fur of badger, pijicki, mink even, for the wind is sharp and the water splashes and your pink stockings aren't much to be proud of. But I know that you conceal another pair of pink stockings in your bag and that, under the black satin or nigger velvet, there's a butterfly-wing tunic, low-necked and sleeveless.

Spring is here. If it's fine you'll be able, around eleven, to put on your bright sandals and flowered dress—under what new uniform coat?—the dress in which you'll dine tonight, you elegant ones who expect me to call you thrifty. Thrifty? Pah!... Lazy....

Excursions

You called on me this afternoon, my young friend. And you said, as you sent your little brimless felt hat flying with a flick, as a clown does his wig when he comes to bow to his audience : 'I'll pick you up tomorrow morning! Be ready at seven and leave things to me. We'll lunch at B. . . at midday on the dot. We'll have a snack at C. . . at four. And may my tongue be covered with ulcers if half past seven doesn't find us at D. . . , elbows on the table, with an aperitif!'

Your arm pointed through the open window to your smart eleven horsepower alongside the pavement, coachwork in expensive wood, nickelled prow, stern inlaid with mahogany and rosewood. I know from experience that this outstretched arm holds the steering-wheel firmly and that this hand, freckled and hardened since the spring, could not possibly, from timidity or rashness, contravene any paragraph of the highway code. All the same, I shan't obey the gesture of this hand. It's not with you I'll travel, my young friend. You'll wrinkle up your small unpowdered nose and reply : 'You *are* difficult!' Well, you've hit on the right word, I *am* difficult. You're perfect on a trip, but I want both more and less than perfection, something other than your inexorable time-tables, which put to shame the ambitions of a railway system.

You are a young woman of twenty-six or twenty-eight. It's the misfortune and the good luck of women of your generation to have experienced everything at your age, even suffering. War made you wise, love saw you tremble. Modern education has also taught you to travel, if by travelling is meant covering long distances, and at sixteen you were able, unembarrassed, to settle hotel bills single-handed, tips included. The disdain of the *blasé*, the omniscience of the rich, these were your lot from your first communion. You don't hesitate, you don't dawdle. When you're seated at the steering-wheel you yield with dignity the right of way both to monster cars and to those buzzing insects of the road, a sort of terrible harvest-bug, small and generally scarlet, wingless creatures, whose passage strikes terror. You brush certain small vehicles with your wing in order to teach them to have respect for a straight line. And you decipher maps with such a virtuoso air that I always expect, as you unfold the thousand-square hectares' sheet, to hear you vocalize the *cavatina* 'Paris-Biarritz' or the scale of the hills and slopes of Nîmes-Le Havre.

You know the villages, their resources and their pitfalls. You are not imposed on by the 'hostelry', furnished in the ancient style, for the salad is no better served in an old chipped Rouen *jardinière*, or the fruit salad in a warming-pan deflected from its proper usage. You are, I repeat, perfect; I shan't travel with you. I've too many defects, let alone that of no longer being your age. The ribbon of the road, the woods and fields that flank it, no longer appeal to me when they are half-obliterated by speed. And I know that, in our epoch, there is only one luxury—to be dilatory, only one aristocracy—leisure. So leave without me and speed the summer long, impassive and undazzled, at a 'good' average of eighty. For my part, I'll go away and I wager that you won't join me. You are like the greyhound, Lola, who couldn't run with the little bulldogs because in three bounds she had reached the horizon and was searching everywhere for the winded bulldogs she had passed without seeing. Space is yours; leave me what is more beautiful : the woods of scattered pines, the stream turning and twisting in the trough of its valley, the pink foxgloves ranged between the domes of the charcoal furnaces, the brown bread taken from the oven as I pass, with its smell that excites hunger and sleep; the sandpit with purple heather, the lake guessed at behind the hedges—or was it perhaps a field of blue-flowered flax?—the paddocks planted with hemp, drowsy with the flight of butterflies . . . and much more beside, even more irresistible. All this is mine, together with the rural silence, varied and accessible, that you can't hear; for nothing halts you on the road as you plunge through the smoke of the bakehouse fire and transfix the butterflies' flight, you who told me that day when I wanted to sleep on the moving velvet of a sandpit : 'Don't be childish !'

Soon, one of the very smallest motor-cars will be taking me away. Do you want to place yourself at my disposal for my kind of trip? Don't worry about me, I beg you. Yes, I'll have a can of petrol in the boot, and four new sparking-plugs. But, most important, I'll have a thick rug, some Gruyère cheese, some duck *pâté*, fat roast pork in its own jelly, fruit, a flask of good wine, some hot coffee. So provisioned, I shall travel fifty or five hundred kilometres from Paris. I've learned from experience that the summer nights are short and mild, and that the red streak heralding the dawn tinges the sky with a light so severe as to wring the heart. But it's a moment so pure that one savours in it the joy of thinking of nothing and no one, except childhood. Even should you pass, at daybreak, on the road you would go on your way ignorant that I had slept there at the edge of the wood in the most sumptuous solitude, that I'd just awoken under the sad dawn, moistened with a niggardly dew that is dried up, drop by drop, by the black fan of the pines.

Captive Gardens

Two months ago my neighbour was jealous of my yellow laburnum and then of my wistaria, vigorous even in its youth, that throws from wall to lime-tree, from lime to the climbing roses, its snake-like shoots dripping with mauve clusters and heavy with perfume. But at the same time I cast an envious look at his double-flowering cherries; and, with July here, how to compete with his geraniums? At full noon their red velvet achieves an indescribable violet, mysteriously evoked by the vertical light. . . . Patience! He'll see my purple sage in October and November, my neighbour will.

And, without having to wait, he can always catch sight of those ambitious crossed poles that I dignify with the title 'rose-pergola', the heavy clumps of roses, capsized like drunken heads. I have left for my other neighbour the shade flowers, the clematis as blue as it is violet, the lilies of the valley, the begonias made blowzy by an hour's sunshine. An old garden nearby nurtures a giant mallow to which the rest of the plant kingdom has been sacrificed; ancient and untiring, it bears a dazzle of blossoms, pink when they open, mauve as they fade. A little farther away flames the red hawthorn, glory of the Breton spring, and a bushy vine, arranged like a mosaic on the façade of a small mansion, appeases with its vertical lawns the rustic taste of an inhabitant of Auteuil whose land has only the width and breadth of an orange-box. Friendly rivalry that summons old folk and well-conducted children to the threshold of these captive gardens, brandishing of rakes and hoes, clashing of curved beaks of secateurs, truck-garden odour of manure and mown grass, how much longer can you save Paris from the mournful cubism, the rectangular shadow of apartment blocks? Every month in the 16th *arrondissement* sees the felling of an avenue of limes, a thicket of spindle-trees, an old-fashioned arbour rounded to the measure of the crinoline.

On my outer boulevard, drowned in foliage, there has risen in six months a block of flats with the shape and self-importance of a glaring new tooth. A charming low dwelling, content for a hundred years to flourish in the middle of its garden like a sitting hen on its nest of straw, has now—flanked by seven new storeys—lost for ever its right to the sun, its scarab-coloured mornings, its fiery grave sunsets. It stays mute and frozen like an extinct planet, clad in its own mourning.

Our captive gardens can be saved now only by foreign money. A millionaire from far away may chance to become infatuated

with a begardened mansion in an old district. Then he purchases
it and improves it. He says: 'I'd like two or three others like this',
in his grand conception; or else explains: 'It's for tennis.' But let
us do him the justice to admit that at times he placards his dislike
of tennis and his enthusiasm for everything to do with France's
past. It's thanks to him that, on some extensively cleared and
regally enlarged piece of land, there confront each other Gothic
village churches assembled stone by stone like jigsaw puzzles,
Basque terraces, a faithfully scaled-down Norman orchard, court-
yards of little low funereal box-trees from the Midi and some
Breton thatched cottage, not to mention an antique theatre. A
collection made in rather puerile taste but which touches us pro-
vincials, shrinking prisoners of Paris, we who tremble at the fall
of a lilac or the lopping of a chestnut, who inhabit the shore of a
tide of building that nibbles at and encroaches on the Bois, who
fervently defend our narrow allotment of greenery. What still
remains, deserves to be sung in a melancholy key. Boylesve recalls
a garden destroyed. Abel Hermant, though still in possession,
already mourns the stately unfolding of the spring under his
balcony, two steps from the Madeleine.

The Duchess of Sforza grows her Morère strawberries between
the pillars of a balcony in the avenue Henri-Martin, and Philippe
Berthelot can see the cherries ripen on his grafted trees in the
boulevard du Montparnasse. Behold, at the quai Saint-Michel, the
garden raised on a roof! On the quai Malaquais, Albert Flament
guards his souvenirs of Florence within four walls, in the midst
of a cool and charming courtyard where rounded cypresses and
box-trees are rooted in a mosaic setting. In the rue Jacob, Gourmont's 'Amazon'* fails to make the dried-up plot blossom, un-
visited by the sun. But the fine anaemic grass that grows there in
the shade is welcome to the nocturnal cat, and the screech-owl
perches, in literary style, on a dead tree draped with a rag of
ivy. . . . It doesn't need much of a vine on a wall to comfort a
glance that goes from white paper to window, from window to
white paper. . . .

---

* Rémy de Gourmont (1858–1915), symbolist essayist and critic. His
Letters to the Amazon were addressed to the American Natalie Clifford
Barney, a friend of his last years.

An open doorway, in a seemingly no-account street, one day revealed to me a kind of deep provincial paradise, adorned with ancient weeping ash-trees, magnolias, stone vases, sleeping cats, and even apple-trees in cordons, planted in palisade around the lawn. . . . Apple-trees in cordons. . . . O you bucolic Parisians, decked in May with lilies of the valley, gatherers of lilac, you who go into ecstasies over a tuft of grass or a snowdrop, aren't you the guardians of Paris's remaining rural secrets? Apple-trees in cordons. . . .

Holidays

The hot weather, the mid-year three months' flowering, is theirs at last. For six months family negotiations have revolved around some near-inaccessible oasis. Dates, budgetary manipulations, vehicular planning, all have converged on holidays. Our children have suffered the resentment of schooldays in June, the tiresome overall with its sleeve sticking to the small damp arm; they have braced their failing young spirits in the general afternoon somnolence—all the desires and intentions of ten parents are subjugated to the 'little one's holiday' as a just reward.

Children of Paris, even those of you whom maternal solicitude exiles from Paris to the care of suburban schools, you've long deserved your annual reward.

June has passed, with its roses and strawberries. Bagatelle has blazed, its every rose-bush afire. Every empty nest testifies to a thousand flights. Children, you raised your heads to sniff the breeze like jaded colts when July brought through the open windows of your prisons the call of the resin-exuding pines and the shaven lawns.

It's a hard, uncaring rule that keeps children and adolescents seated studiously before note-pad or a textbook at 30 degrees centigrade. . . .

Now our children are free. See them, in the river or on some seashore's eroded strand, naked or as near as makes no difference. Their elegance is in that bloom like the blushing cheek of a nectarine, that fine dry knee, that shoulder endowed with a sudden feminine smoothness since last year. The shoulder-strap of last year's old swimsuit stretches and breaks, the edge of the short trunks is taut against the muscles produced by twelve months of growth.

My astonished daughter regards her last year's slough; the young snake stifles in the skin that it had abandoned on the Breton sands, that other August. 'In 1924 I came up to here,' she says, placing the flat of her hand under her chin. She feels some pride at this, and a little embarrassment. 'Oh, I can't get through the gap in the fence any more,' she announces. A tear even swells on the fresh, lash-guarded margin of her fine eyelids : 'Oh, my little blue sweater ! . . .' 'But you can get another one.' 'Yes . . . but it won't be my little blue sweater any more ! . . .'

Must she, at twelve, impelled by growth like all that's shooting up, must she already experience the sorrows of growing older, lament for the time she no longer possesses?

I don't like to see her sentimental, moved by a memory, vulnerable to a sound, a colour, a scent inhaled, that she recognizes. Doesn't she still know how to assail fiercely the rocks, how to watch for the flotsam of wrecks and snatch it from the waves? It's one thing for a child to screw up her eyes and announce, like a herald, in a shrill voice : 'The steamer from Granville ! The two o'clock plane ! A curlew, Mama, a curlew !' It's quite another to stay idly silent, with mouth half-open and bemused eye. Premature reverie is disquieting for observers. How can one not be anxious? The eyelashes flicker feebly over the dazed pupils; but this countenance, so soon visited by so much grace, reveals no ecstasy to greet the immense marine light. A formidable quietude, a boundless expectancy. Alas! She has dropped her unwanted toys at her feet.

Presently I'll take her to Saint-Malo; along the way we'll rediscover, she and I, the holidays of childhood, the handful of sweets proffered by the village grocer, the new-laid egg from the nearest farm, the bowl of milk, the peach firm under its velvet skin, all those gifts, all the homage paid to the arrogant little barefooted queen.

In town again, my daughter will still despise the children playing on the beach '*en chapeau*' and the small girls dressed as young damsels. 'Can't they dress like boys, like everyone else?' But she doesn't fail to display a new and strange mechanical knowledge as she studies the cars that pass on the Sillon. 'When *I* drive. . . . How wretched to see a fine X. . . chassis with such coachwork! I can't imagine what they can have been thinking of!' And to turn to me, astounded, over the young garage fledgling I've managed to hatch out. . . .

As before, the dressmaker will throw some striped rag over her shoulder. But I'll wait in vain for the circus-urchin gesture with which she was wont to tie a strip of cotton round her forehead, unless she proudly drapes it round her bare bronzed thigh. Just now she arranges herself like a model, tucks in her backside, juts out a hip and murmurs: 'Let's try it with the waist a bit higher. . . .' She looks for a mirror, no longer for a bandeau of bright shreds. And, leaving the *pâtisserie*, she's both gauche and graceful, collides with a table, raises an eyebrow, bites her lip, blushes at last like a dark rose, all because a young man steps aside to open the door for her, saying: 'After you, Mademoiselle. . . .'

Grape Harvesters

'Where will you go this September?' my friend Valentine asked me in May. I feel slightly guilty whenever she questions me. She asks questions easily and expertly. She disturbs me with her knowledge of the future, immediate or remote. She fixes a point in the future and there one is, at spa, Saint-Moritz or Rome. Six months before the event she announces: 'On the afternoon of 14th January I shall be having tea at Caux.'

'September? September, hmm. . . . Let's see, it's high tide at full moon. . . . I shan't budge from here because of the fishing, because the equinoctial gale will be superb. . . .'

My friend Valentine shrugs her thin, even somewhat scrawny, shoulders. Her whole body is possessed by a sour youthfulness, as if devastated by unending adolescence. Seen from behind in the street she seems, like so many women nowadays, to be ten or twelve years old. Face to face she seems weary of having acted the little girl so long. So what? What will be, will be. So, in May, she shrugged her shoulders, draped in transparent organdie.

See her now, after a most cultivated Parisian summer. She has 'done' the decorative arts, dined on the *quais*, kept open house till 1st August, lunched in the gardens of the 17th *arrondissement*. She doesn't pay me a visit, she drops in while passing. A small white hat, a dress of white, black and green—what's she looking round for, her umbrella? No, her motoring coat. It's been left outside, on the road, in the car, the car that's out of sight; it's smart to drop in on a friend *en passant*, four hundred kilometres from Paris, as if one had walked all the way. . . . At the bottom of the meadow the sea, with courteous tongue, moistens the iron foliage and fiery flowers of the cardoons. But my friend Valentine doesn't notice the sea, or the beach, or the summer-stripped headland, brown and yellow as a deer; she's thinking of grape-harvesting. For two or three years now the grape harvest has been as assiduously cultivated as cashmere. Between my friend Valentine and the calm milky sea there interposes, incongruously, a picture of grape-harvesting endowed with an arbitrary charm, and I pity this young woman constrained by Fashion to endless anticipation. Thus it is that in winter's frosts the *couturier* must deal with crêpe and embroidered wild flowers, drape swathes of fur in the dog-days. . . .

'You'll be going to harvest, then, Valentine?'

'Of course, my dear.'

'Is it the first time?'

She blushes.

'Yes . . . that is . . . I was to have harvested last year on the estate of my friends X. . . , and two years ago, even at . . .'

'Don't make excuses. And what sort of harvesting get-up do you envisage?'

'Violet-purple cretonne printed with yellow grapes,' retorts my friend straight off.

'Hat?'

'Yellow. A violet ribbon tied under the chin.'

'Shoes?'

'Plaited. In yellow and white kid.'

'Scissors?'

'Like a stork's beak. I found some ravishing ones at Strasbourg.'

Can't I catch her out? She's even thought of scissors! I'm amazed to find that her ignorance of natural things stands her in almost as good stead as consummate experience—except in actual practice. She characterizes the season by the material, sport by the equipment, female beauty by jewellery. She interprets the language of symbols like a romantic sweetheart, in fact. . . . But I shan't tell her so, it would certainly hurt her feelings.

'You know, Valentine, you can do without scissors if you like.'

My friend's plucked eyebrows rose in astonishment and disappeared under the little chalk-white hat.

'Do without! When I've an antique steel chain to hang them from my belt!'

'. . . It's up to you,' I say. 'You see, the stalk of each bunch at an inch or two from the parent stock is swollen like a snake that hasn't yet digested its meal. If you press with your nail on this barely visible swelling it breaks like glass, and the bunch falls into the basket held out by your other hand. It's a little peasant trick I'm teaching you, Valentine, so that you can fill your basket faster. . . . That's how I used to manage, in 1917. . . .'

To be sure, the rest was none of her business. Those wartime harvests belong only to my memories. Red earth baked by long sunny days, a broiling September moistened with dew at dawn, unexpected bunches beneath the fig-trees smelling of fresh milk. . . . That year the sky distilled a flawless blue from pink dawn to pinker evening. Never were there so many peaches on the peach-trees, screening, when ripe, the vines; never were there so many yellow plums and greengages mingled with the vine-tendrils. So many kingfishers gleaming over the river, so many bees in harmonious aureoles around the limes, so many shrilling swallows piercing the clouds of midges. . . . So much animal joy and unresponsive vegetable luxuriance at our silent harvestings. . . .

Women's hands, children's hands turned back the foliage, handled and cut the warm grapes. There was not a man to be seen between the parallel rows of vines. The males spared by the war were those under seventeen or over fifty; these carried with bowed back, from vine to vats, the wooden containers that weigh, full, half a quintal or more.

Towards noon a young woman emerged from the vines, ran on to the path, sat down in the shade of a fig-tree, and picked up a child fastened in swaddling clothes. Her milk was urgent and while she freed and woke the nurseling I saw mingled drops of milk and tears falling on the child from the mute and solitary harvester.

Fur and Feather

The year has started well for huntsmen. A premature abundance of game, and by no means of the smallest, set the hardy trackers of Paris afoot from August onward. The 16th *arrondissement* held the record for a time with its leopard, and its kill in the boulevard Lannes. But furred and feathered creatures were brought down, in emulation, on every side. Two foxes, one of which installed itself in the preserves of the Opéra, an 'unknown' bird resembling 'a large turkey-cock with flattened beak', another bird, equally devoid of pedigree, black, immense, that inspired terror—but why?—in flying away, a lion cub, a magnificent release of exotic birds beneath the glass roof of the gare du Nord. . . . I give up. The fauna of Paris, these recent months, defy the imagination.

Among others, what is one to make of the hornbill and the white-throated laughing thrush? Never fear, the laughing thrush heralded in September, flew timidly enough and meant its tormentors no harm.

The 16th *arrondissement*, my own, does not fail to offer the student several interesting examples of European fauna. One night I found by the gate of my small garden a pretty white cow that I might easily have captured. I know now that the nocturnal white cow allows one to approach, accepts water in a bucket and salt from an outstretched hand. The twilight ewe possesses the same peculiarities, as observed by me in a ewe recumbent by the side of the outer boulevard. Perhaps these remarks may serve for a treatise on Parisian venery. A panther from the Chad, captured with the aid of Philippe Berthelot in a staff-room at the Foreign Office, brightened my stay for a time. But I implore you to believe that I would not countenance the inexcusable negligence of a menagerie proprietor who allowed it to slouch about on the pavement, or in the weighing-in enclosure at Auteuil, or among my neighbours' flower-beds and rose-gardens. Its beautiful coat, its golden-amber eyes, its confident deerlike grace and gentle friendly call, these I would cherish, aware that the urban scalp-hunters are in earnest and that all is fair for them on the warpath : the Browning, the halberd, the tomahawk, the slingshot, and asphyxiating gases.

They needn't count on me, these decimators of partridges, pond-frogs and hornbills, to inform them when, and in what part of the Bois, I spy—without any evil intent—a small mysterious animal that warms itself, autumn and spring, in the length of a ray of sunlight that slants across a path. I confirm that it is chestnut, smooth-coated, shorter and chunkier than the common marten, lacking the dash of a squirrel. My bitches know it, it flees from prudence rather than fear and disappears into a lair burrowed in the very slope of the old fortifications. It is always alone, and old perhaps. Its life is a wretched little life. . . . But perhaps I've said too much already. Perhaps, in my imprudence, I may have brought about a militarily organized *battue* in the copses of Auteuil.

As I write there take place the pursuit, wounding and killing of the plump partridge, noisier in full flight than an aeroplane, the unreflecting quail, the pheasant that ornaments the trees it roosts in. The hare's heart beats fit to burst, even the night brings no respite for the smallest trembling game. The fashion journals promote a hundred different outfits for huntresses, with an illustration alongside the text showing that the huntress of 1925 is no improvement on that of 1924. Without bust or buttocks she stands heronlike, yet endowed with an interminable bosom. If I am to believe these facile designers, the huntress is shod with dainty pumps or high boots in soft leather. She is armed with a carbine as long as a boat-hook, a powder-puff, a cigarette, and a wrist-watch that points, no doubt, to the last hour of the nearest marksman. She is patterned with great checks, like a bathroom, or wears an old warrior's stripes. Beneath her masculine cravat she wears a blouse of white *crêpe de Chine*, ensuring—God willing—that the game can spy her from afar. Well, well, if I can believe the facile designers, the huntress on foot is a brave little creature who wouldn't harm a dove, even with a rifle.

But as for the woman who goes in for big-game hunting, I maintain the most malevolent silence on the subject. May the powerful dry foot of the stag, slain among the tears it has shed, may the small delicate hoof of the roe-deer, brought in with gaping throat and dangling neck like a murdered child, return at night to trouble her dreams for ever—it is all she deserves.

A friend of mine, a literary young man with plenty of talent, had been used to hunting from infancy, and with all the rage of a bloodthirsty child. He hunts no longer. I evinced my surprise and asked the reason for this sensible behaviour. He hesitated only a moment before telling me this: 'I was shooting partridges last year in Brittany. I wounded one, which still fluttered and hid behind a bush; but I had marked it well and felt sure of getting hold of it. I reached the bush, pulled up against a low fence, and encountered a little grey-bearded man on the farther side. The old gentleman was holding my wounded partridge in his hands, caressing its beating wing and its frantic little head. I told him that . . . that I had shot the partridge in the open field, that it had originally fallen on the stubble, that . . . well, that was all there was to be said! He continued to caress the partridge and seemed not to understand me. Finally he raised his head and asked me in the most moderate tones: "Sir, have you ever thought that one day, in this world or another, you might be the game in your turn?" I tell you, it affected me so strangely, that little phrase, that ever since I've lost all inclination to hunt. . . .'

Fads and Fashions

Jewellery in Peril

The year will end uneasily. How many women are pondering as they fiddle with the 'idle capital' on their fingers. Never have they felt so directly menaced. And yet silk costs as much as woven hair, raw yarn doesn't lag behind silk, the smallest piece of kid-leather, shaped more or less like a foot, costs three hundred francs. And pears and apples desert the modest table, already abandoned by the leg of mutton, and women—even those who survive on toast and a cup of tea—have already voiced their loud, ravenous clamour. . . .

But the threat of a particular tax finds them dumb, full of rancour and scheming. They are not going to be had so easily. The dramatic *dénouement* is their familiar element. You'll see, these apparently imprudent ones will give men one more surprise. Already, one who is garlanded, sleeping and waking, with a row of incomparable and inseparable pearls, a necklace she fondles and kisses, already this fetishist loses fervour, speaks of her necklace with a waning passion. 'You know, it would cost me something like thirty thousand francs a year for the pleasure of keeping a necklace of this value. . . . Thirty thousand francs! The rent of a good apartment. . . . The price of a small property! Do you understand. . . ?' We understand. We go further and understand clearly that woman, surprising creature who blends poet, starling and perfect lawyer, doesn't want to pay more than once for her pleasures and won't agree to pay rent for her luxuries.

Perhaps in every woman there is a businessman. This has, rather unkindly, been stated more than once already. Happy or unhappy, this businessman, engaged with dress, art, life, even science, seems to be roused by certain sounds—of coin, of safe deposits, of prattled figures; he dreams with ear pricked like a war-horse when the breeze brings bursts of martial music. . . . The words 'a tax on idle capital' arouse woman from a frivolous dream. Where she was prodigal she has turned rapacious, once scatter-brained she is defiant and calculating. . . .

Fine jewels, family heirlooms, birthday gewgaws and New Year surprises, already you are weighed, your value calculated, your limpid clarity attracts a legatee's glances. The same proud mouth that once announced 'They're worth so much!' now murmurs: 'They'll cost me so much.'

I suppose that this misfortune will see the triumphant renaissance of the once so pretentious, so-called 'artistic' jewellery, to the profit of exoticism. Already the heavy necklace of Peking glass finds favour. It is blue, green or yellow, translucent or veiled with milky flecks. The rounded beads, save when shaped like nasturtium seeds they imitate the Oriental emerald, delight us with their periwinkle blue. Their compressed substance seems moist; they play happily on the brown skin where each bead trails behind it, in place of shadow, a little spot of bluish light.

I know a Chinese necklace of green glass, long and heavy as a slave's chain, that burdens as well as adorns a charming neck. It is as green as a frog, as blatantly green as royal jade. Czechoslovak glassware cannot match these refined barbarities, also fashioned in thick circlets round the arm, tinkling like bronze cow-bells. The vogue for Chinese necklaces and bracelets has only just begun and we are barely acquainted with those whose crystalline substance conceals—competing with the overesteemed 'sulphurs'—a little pink and green snake, a twist of gold powder. . . . It's not that they're beautiful, but that they come from afar. And then they are all, like the necklaces, the constructs of sphere and circumference, and this eternal simplicity is no negligible magic. If the pearl had been created studded with facets, it would be able to laugh at this famous tax. A cut rock crystal appeals to us less than a perfect sphere, smooth to the touch, transparent, impenetrable, that mirrors every terrestrial image on its surface, fantastically distorts them and turns them into sorcery. . . .

No tax threatens the necklaces, all blue, Chinese, that tinkle from my neck to my knees. Other worlds, virgin and multi-coloured, roll in a casket that I can open without fear of tax demands. These spheres have their history.

After the war our children searched in vain—and still search— for glass marbles. To satisfy my daughter, one day I wrote to the master of Fire and Glass, the creator of the marvellous Fountain, to Lalique in fact, and asked him : 'What has become of our children's glass marbles?' Lalique offered no explanation. A few weeks later I received a hundred marbles from Lalique—pink, red, opalescent, blue as the flame that saw their birth, green as grapes, as waves, as silvered absinthe.

But—and here you see the extent of childish deprivation and maternal selfishness—it was I who kept the precious 'taws' in a casket and my daughter Bel-Gazou still hasn't got her glass marbles.

Too Short

Too short, gentlemen, too short. I write 'gentlemen' since few women make it their profession to dress women. They are in a minority, a minority of rare quality that readily gains acceptance, but a minority. An habitual shamelessness leads women to prefer a salesman to retail the sheer stockings, the mesh of which, stretched over a man's hand—'See how very flattering to the thigh this stocking is, Madame'—reveals all its delicacy. It seems that a masculine arm is the best measure for Valenciennes lace and for ribbon. . . . We speak of the embroiderer, the cutter, the milliner, the hosier, as masculine. We say 'the *couturier*', using the male gender, even when the *couturier* walks on two feet shod with brocade and paste jewellery and adorns her swanlike neck with two million francs' worth of pearls. . . . Well, *Couturier*, great *Couturier*, trousered or skirted, I tell you to your face : this year again, it's too short.

All very well for the walking costume, so named by antithesis, since its skirt hobbles the legs, pulls the knees together, wears out the stockings and hinders walking. Shortened, it gives the stationary woman a pretty little alert air which she loses as soon as she begins to walk—but what need to begin walking? The elegant 'walking costume' does not ambulate. If we want to get about, on foot or on horseback, climb a mountain or traverse a marsh, it won't be you, *Couturier*, that we'll consult, but specialists that you despise, the technicians of the waterproof raincoat, the puttee, the ski-boot and the Saumur riding-breeches. *Your* walking outfit covers four hundred yards between midday and one o'clock and that's quite enough for the delicate stitched kid-leather that your accomplice, the expert in footwear, calls his *matinée* shoes. So cut it at knee-level if you like, or higher still. But this year you have shortened both the afternoon and the evening gown. A scissor-slash of some importance, after which the exertions of the embroiderer, the ingenuity and luxury of the weaver, go un-rewarded. It's in vain that you hang on your clients' backs a loose panel, billowed up by the least movement; in vain that you dust an already silvered veil with seven hundred thousand little stars; in vain that you 'cheat', attaching a *lamé*, pleated, embroidered, fringed train that sweeps the carpet, slender guy-rope of a tunic suspended sixteen inches higher. . . . It's in vain that you scatter suns, rockets, palms, fountains, roses over the flat stomach, the illusory backside and steppe-like bosom of the Peri of 1924; your evening gown, your full-dress rig-out resemble some abortive project, a novel minus a *dénouement*, an ostrich that has moulted, an idyll without poetry. Too many feet, too many feet, and not enough material!

I am told, O great *Couturier*, that you easily lose your temper and that your first word will be to tell me to mind my own business. That's just because you're not accustomed to criticism. Your art—which has a turnover of as many millions as the cinema—is content, with singular modesty, with 'communiqués' and provides an income for those two second-rate bards, the public relations officer and the official reporter. But no one treats your work, as it so often deserves, like a fine painting, like an enamel, a new novel, a stage play, like a ceramic. . . .

Whose fault is this? Up to now your petty tyranny has admitted only paid hirelings. You deserve less 'fixing' and more considera-tion, you surely deserve that I should give myself the pleasure of coming to you, seeing what you create, saying what I think of it and going away again—in my nice little dress that hasn't your trademark.

In one month I have already seen two hundred dresses on parade. At the opening of a new season this is an instructive as well as amusing parade. I learned there this year's way of carrying one's stomach which, though flat, retains a shieldlike arrogance and sways forward and back, backwards and forwards. Where is the Spanish or Martinique hip-rolling of the models of 1914? All very well to talk of hips, we don't bulge at the sides any more! It was there I learned that 'the waistline is rising'. I'll say it's rising, as far as the navel, and doesn't hesitate to descend much lower, much, much lower. Then again, the length of the back is startling, if I can call this flat parallelogram, with a skirt fit for a little girl of ten hanging at the end, a back. 'Three inches of legs and right on to the back.' Oh, that back! Thirty inches of back, without pleat or fold. Smile, Mr Embroiderer, this is where you can let yourself go. Embroider, on this vertiginous back, pagodas, fruit, Arabic numerals, rural scenes, Pompeian friezes and automobiles. But your smile is sickly, Embroiderer. And with reason. The Weaver, who is a genius, has got it into his head that he can manage without you and he weaves marvellously. In relief, in depth, silky, ribbed, variegated, pale as the shadow of smoke, vigorous as the summer foliage in an avenue, he executes his arabesques on every material and defies you. Get cracking, Embroiderer, and improvise, you too.

Two hundred dresses! O great *Couturier*, you've shown me them in every shade. They bear charming names—you're not short of affectation, great *Couturier*, nor of a sense of the ridiculous, or phrases. Blessings on you this year for bringing blue back into fashion. The long-banished blue reappears, interposed between violet and purple, and the eye bathes in it happily, suddenly aware that happiness is incomplete without the savour of blue. Black competes with the entire rainbow, calling to its aid the pink of a half-glimpsed breast, the gleam of an arm or leg under lace: 'Don't forget that I am not only distinguished, noble, sumptuous, but also the most voluptuous of all, and the most satanic,' insinuates black. Above all others I find this prince of darkness too short—like its seven comrades, despite their divided trains that sweep the ground, get caught up in doors, twine round the legs of chests and firmly swathe the feet of armchairs.

Too short, this fake libertine mourning in soubrette's skirt; too
short, this gauze-winged dream that doesn't conceal its attach-
ments to earth!

Great *Couturier*, do you recall an evening when you showed
us, after truncated Salammbos, abbreviated Mélusines, sirens
treated like Alcibiades' dog, and many a ravishing 'little model'
with low waist and high hemline which I privately christened 'the
fiancée of the legless cripple'—do you recall showing us a bridal
robe loaded with pearls, a long, long robe which descended above
invisible feet the steps of your 'presentation stage'? It descended,
gliding as if by magic. Six yards of train followed, lace and tulle
frothing over its still, calm water. . . . Didn't the cry of admiration
that burst forth at this sight, great *Couturier*, resound in your ears
like a warning, or at least a piece of advice? No? So much the
worse.

Underneath

'This way, Madame!' said the elderly saleswoman. She barred
my entry to the little trying-on room, closed by a velvet curtain,
which I was about to penetrate, and led me smilingly to the opposite end of the establishment.

'There now! We're better off here, aren't we? It's more
homely.'

I did not share her opinion. The homeliness in question was
that of a sort of vestibule-cum-drawing-room between two glass
swing-doors, afflicted by piercing draughts, with a gloomy light
falling from above.

'If you've no space for a fitting, Madame R., why don't you
just admit "I've no room"?'

'Oh Lord! What must you think of me!'. . .

She raised her wrinkled hands with their painted nails and I heard the bracelets of ebony, hollow gold and good imitation jade clash as they slid down her forearms. Her wise, wrinkled eyes sought the ceiling, then returned to mine without insistence and she smiled showing all her teeth, one of them—of pure metal— gleaming.

'You're teasing, Madame. One should never tell you anything but the truth. And you know, telling a client the truth produces a strange sensation, as if one were doing something one shouldn't. The truth, Madame, is that I have three empty salons in the long gallery, but. . . . Oh Lord! . . .'

The bracelets clashed and Madame R. pirouetted on her well-shod little feet. She is sixty-four, with hair dyed a dark red and the outline of a young girl. She conceals neither her age nor her wrinkles, which she makes up with bright rouge. Under the rouge, the powder, the bracelets, the short black dress with its two panels, there is nevertheless a shrewd old woman who succeeds in resembling neither a procuress nor a mad grandmother. She is, dare I say, a born saleswoman. She might have managed a dress-making establishment had she not lacked a kind of cruel severity and the wish to dominate. Her gift lies in finesse, and only finesse. She loves the long, empty hours, the bustle, the luxurious salons. She likes irony, scandalmongering, a piece of chocolate at four o'clock, the hidden cigarette, the bag of cherries. She 'earns well' and feeds her family well, a solemn family in sombre woollens from which she escapes every morning, concealing her private delight from herself. . . .

'You'll scold me, Madame!' she whispered with a contrite grimace that gathered the lax skin of her neck in convergent folds under her chin. 'Yes, I do have empty salons! Yes, I have brought you to this draughty corner! It's very wicked! But . . . but I couldn't stand it any longer down there!'

'You couldn't stand what?'

She closed her black-rimmed eyes, painfully swallowed her saliva like a choking hen, and whispered in my ear a single word, revolting and mysterious: 'The smell.'

Then she fluttered from one door to the other, cried sharply: 'Mademoiselle Cécile, you're making fun of everyone!'; languidly demanded: 'Mademoiselle Andrée, when you're ready,

Madame Colette's three-piece!' and cast off from a chair, so that I might sit down, a cloak of gold, moonlight and purple tissue which she trod underfoot like a queen. She 'played for time' like a good actress and let me meditate on the word, the word full of vague horror and fascination. . . .

'The smell of what, Madame R.?'

She did not keep me waiting but retorted in the plain language of an aristocrat: 'Why, the smell of hairy women, then!'

'How so? Is X. . . dressing a revue then?'

Madame R. simpered, suddenly prudish.

'The house of X. . . only dresses the right people, as you know perfectly well. The right people—and artistes, of course.'

She dropped her voice into a more serious register, rounding her eyes like an impassioned preacher: 'About the smell, Madame, I retract nothing! I've said what I've said! I'd repeat it under the knife! I'm old enough to remember a time when one could enter the salons of the House of X. . . at any time without breathing any odour but the scent of corylopsis and ylang-ylang. Perhaps there were times when there was an excessive odour of sanctity, but still. . . . Nowadays, Madame, it smells of a steam-bath here, a steam-bath!'

She seized a snippet of *lamé* caught between two wardrobe doors and used it as a fan, closing her tragic eyelids as if to say 'I've said too much. I give up'. But, since I kept silent, she re-opened her eyes precipitately and said hastily: 'What can you expect, Madame? Once a woman used to wear underwear, fine linen underwear that cleansed her skin; now, when she takes off her dress, turning it inside-out like skinning a rabbit, what do you see? A long-distance walker, Madame, in a little pair of trunks. A baker's assistant in bakehouse get-up. No chemise, no linen drawers, no petticoat, no combinations, a brassière sometimes, yes, often a brassière. . . . Before coming for a fitting these ladies have walked, danced, eaten, perspired . . . I'll say no more. . . . It's a long time from their morning bath! And their dress, worn next to the skin, what does it smell of, their dress that cost two thousand smackers? Of a boxing-match, Madame, a fencing championship! *Twelfth round*, unpleasant smell. . . . Oh Lord!'

She exhibited the hand-clasping, the affected declamation,

acquired like a tic by women who often meet men who imitate women. But her disgust seemed genuine and her nostrils were pale. I recalled the phobia that used to afflict a corset-maker who took all her meals in a restaurant to escape the effluvium that filled her own establishment. . . .

A model appeared, a sort of tall blond boy, hair shorn close on the nape of the neck, coming down over the forehead to eyebrow level. Beneath the flesh-coloured evening dress the minor jutting of two small breasts confirmed her nudity. Unblushingly she lifted her skirt and extracted from her stocking a narrow wisp of fuchsia-coloured gauze to wipe her nose vigorously. Her comic gesture evoked in me the recollection of a rehearsal of a play where the author intended the villain to tear half the clothes off the *ingénue*. In the imagination of the sexagenarian playwright the victim was to remain palpitating for a moment, undone like a spoiled white rose, clasping to herself the scanty lace, the exciting froth of underwear in a snowy cascade. . . . The run-through revealed, not the froth and snow, but little panties in saffron silk net, four taut suspenders, and a portion of saffron chemise marked with a large monogram like the inside of a hat; the stagehands may have guffawed but the author certainly didn't laugh. . . .

The coarse words of Adolphe Willette sounded in my ears like an enraged bumble-bee: 'They have done away with feminine underwear, the vandals! Why, even the butcher knows that a leg of mutton has to be done up with a paper frill!'

Make-up

I ran into my friend Z. . . one morning just when he was pushing open the door—all thick glass and ironwork—of a well-known perfumier.

'I've caught you in the act,' I said to him. 'You've come to buy an expensive phial of those lotions that fashion allows men and are consequently labelled "Gentlemen's socks" or "Unleash the wild beasts!" '

'No,' answered Z. . . . 'Come with me, I've no secrets.'

We proceeded across a vertiginous mosaic that reflected us like a lake, to run aground in a delightful harbour between one blonde saleswoman and another. Amiable rather than pretty, they were worthy representatives of an old French luxury trade, which calls for incense-bearers clothed in black serge, whose pious hands are free of jewellery.

'Give me,' asked Z. . . , 'some lipstick.'

'Which one? The light or the dark? The nasturtium or the creole? There's also our liquid rouge, *The Eternal Wound*, which is very popular.'

Z. . . sat down with a determined air.

'I want all of them. At least, I intend to try them all.'

The less pretty of the two blondes cast down her eyes.

'It isn't possible to try them, sir. You see . . .'

'I do see,' interrupted Z. . . . 'All right, I'll buy all your rouges and then try them.'

Five or six small cylinders of gilt metal and a minute phial were handed over to my friend, on a tall counter covered in suède. Very seriously and with a cynicism I found disconcerting he painted his lips conscientiously.

'You're hideous!' I cried. 'Your clipped moustache over that scarlet mouth . . . have you gone mad?'

He passed his tongue over his lips, bit them, wiped them with his handkerchief, then it was the turn of a nasturtium rouge from which I sensed, at a distance, the bitter smell of banana.

'No good!' complained Z. . . in a low tone; and he wiped away the orange traces of the banana lipstick.

For a moment a dark-red cherry rouge claimed his attention. Musingly, he smacked his lips in gluttonous fashion and murmured : 'Not bad . . . not bad. . . .'

One of the two salesgirls, impassive, gave her opinion : 'May I say that the nasturtium rouge, for your complexion, sir, is the one that . . .'

I didn't wait to hear any more.

'My dear friend,' I said drily to Z. . . , 'I've seen enough. I'm off.'

'Wait just a moment, dear friend, I haven't tried the liquid rouge yet. Miss, what are the ingredients that go into the liquid rouge?'

'It has a base of Oriental roses, sir, with the addition of a touch of essence of cloves. . . .'

'Cloves? Curious. I'm tempted by the cloves. . . . Would you wrap up this lipstick for me too? "Stolen Cherries", if I'm not mistaken. Thank you. My dear Colette, I'm at your disposal, shall we stroll to the end of the avenue?'

Curiosity triumphing over revulsion, I waited for Z. . . and let him walk along with me.

'Fine weather,' he remarked innocently. 'And I'm so pleased with my purchases. My wife will be delighted.'

'They're for her? Why didn't you say so, then?'

'No, my dear. They're for me. This make-up that turns my wife's mouth pimento-red, strawberry, tomato, delights the eyes of those who see her, but . . .'

'But?'

'But it's I who eat them, so to speak. I'm in love with my wife. And she adores me to distraction—but not to the point of offering me an epidermis without powder, a mouth of natural pink. As a young married man I endured the twofold caprice of fashion and my wife. The fresh flower that I kissed, plastered for a whole season with a decomposed violet rouge, exhaled the sickly smell of infusion of violets. One winter I browsed—pouah!—on rancid pink cold cream recommended for chaps. And what can one say about the unpleasant flavour of a certain fiery red, the colour of an irritable urticaria, reserved for fêtes under the chandeliers and for dress-rehearsals? . . . I took the best course. I dodge my unhappiness. Since our conjugal love does not wane, I intend to choose the rods that chastise me and I buy my wife's lipstick myself.'

He sighed, then continued: 'If only, while biting her pretty cheeks, I could remove the bilious-coloured powder that covers them! Under that jaundiced yellow, heightened by an artificial flush, my tooth might rediscover an unsuspected blonde flesh tint —don't you think?—that I may eventually forget . . .'

'But at night, doesn't Marcelle show you her true face, properly washed?'

Z. . . . raised an arm and a stick to heaven.

'Washed! That's not the half of it! Scrubbed, polished, scraped with an ivory spatula, rubbed with an ether swab and boiling water, finally carefully coated with a camphor pomade to prevent wrinkles . . .'

'Camphor?' I interrupted. 'Not that wonderful glycerine cream any more, that Marcelle used to claim was so efficient?'

'Alas, no . . .'

Z. . . . took my arm in conspiratorial fashion: 'Dear friend, would you be very kind and do something for me? Start Marcelle off again on the glycerine cream, which I recall as sugary, even a little vanilla-flavoured. It's certainly time. Because I'm afraid. I'm afraid of the mudpack, that blackish rubbish that women plaster their neck and face with, without a quiver or vomiting in disgust. The Great Collector at home, between two linen sheets decked with lace, ah, if you only knew . . .'

'*Manure*—a beauty product!'

With this word, which he accompanied with a bitter grimace, we arrived at the Z's establishment. . . .

'Come up,' said the disturbed husband abruptly. 'My wife gets up late, we'll catch her at her *toilette*. I'm afraid of what may have happened in my absence. . . .'

He had good reason to fear. His charming wife, unrecognizable, was allowing the dregs of a cesspit to dry on her face in a scrupulously evenly applied layer. But she had no time to appear embarrassed, occupied as she was with sharply scolding her little dog.

'Go away, you nasty thing! Hide yourself, you horror! I don't know why I don't send you down to the country! I'll forgive you anything, but not that, d'you hear, not that! . . .'

Magisterially she turned towards me a face encrusted with mud, in which her blue eyes smiled, lotus blossoms of fetid swamps, and explained to me, indicating the dog: 'Just think of it, dear! A little creature I'm so fond of. . . . She's been rolling in something dirty!'

Hats

How are we going to recognize, in thirty years' time, the woman who was so pretty in 1924? I'm very much afraid that we shan't recognize her. Those who were so pretty between 1890 and 1900 announce themselves to us in streets and churches and the theatre, everywhere where, as we say in the Midi, 'one wears a hat'. Would you wager that I could point out to you, among ten or twelve old ladies, the one who was so dreamy and ravishing at twenty and who registered long silences because her silences enhanced her romantic beauty more than words? Her face has renounced everything and her black serge dress smells of the sewing-room, she no longer even thinks of filling in her wrinkles, of powdering them, she does not dye her dusty pepper-and-salt hair. She does not sigh: 'Ah! If you had only seen me. . . .' Only her hat has a delicate mission to fulfil, for, unfashionably, unusually, spread over a light brass framework, the crown very small and the brim very large and wavy, she sports a hood of black lace.

Make no mistake, this is the hat of a twenty-year-old blonde, with blue eyes, whose rather pale mouth and transparent cheek show to advantage under a lace canopy. This is a hat for a day of victory or betrothal, the hat she wore, had copied, adopted, the hat of which she used to say, with an irrefutable air: 'This hat is really me.' She has aged without taking counter-measures—if not, what would her children, her son-in-law, her husband have said? —but not entirely. There are days when she still essays, for the sake of an unknown and stimulating audience, the smile at the corner of the mouth and the haughty gaze that we find so laughable, the smile and the gaze that she had at twenty, with the lace hood.

You are impelled to smile—and I am no better than you—when you meet that other old lady, she who artlessly provokes us with the aggressive felt head-dress, turned up on the left, befeathered on the right, of the Grande Mademoiselle. So decked out she resembles an elderly academician, proud as a monkey. We laugh too soon, before discovering, on her aged face, the relics of one of those militant beauties who affected the plumy feather and the so-called 'musketeer's' asymmetric brim. You may be sure that a timid Areopagus, secretly devoted, named her at the peak of her brilliance 'Bradamante'! The magic of such a name impresses the weak-minded, though the vogue for the ensheathing corsage and the arrogant felt hat passed without Bradamante giving them up.

Today an imploring family still sometimes adjures her 'Look, mother . . . I assure you, grandmother . . .' to return to a sense of reality and she promises to do what they ask. She even visits her dressmaker, 'a remarkably intelligent girl, with a central position, who should have all that's needed to be a success'. She tries on one of the little shapes that current fashion dictates. 'My God, it can't suit me as badly as that. . . .' And then she tries it on again, ridicules her faded countenance, smooths her white hair, claps the little hat on the edge of her forehead once more, frowns, is perplexed, decides at last: 'There, it's not that I don't like it, this little cloche, but it needs . . . you understand, Mademoiselle, the brim isn't quite wide enough for me. Haven't you got a hat a little more . . . a little bigger . . . or, if necessary, you could make it for me specially. Wider, and more—look, a turn-up at the side would show my profile better and we might use something on the right, a—I don't know exactly—an ostrich feather, for instance, to complete the ensemble.'

How shall we recognize, in thirty years' time, the Bradamante of today? Frantic, formal, a prey to dreams but more reverent than her grandmother, she hides, like the hooded Rosalinde of 1885, under the universal cloche. The cloche, I say, the cloche, and still the cloche. Behind, its brim touches the collar of the long jacket or short coat. In front, the brim descends like a visor half-way down the nose. Beneath, the right eye, slightly more obscured than the left, bears the stigma of an arbitrary confinement: it acquires the habit of being a little more closed than the left. Obliged to scrutinize everything with a downward gaze, the women 'bear up into the wind' like badly harnessed horses. Cloche, tailored costume, multicoloured scarf, I was forgetting the stockings the colour of pink gravel. . . .

A young man I once knew made a date with his young woman at the entrance to the Métro and darted forward as soon as he saw her appear, neat in her tailored costume, her neck bound twice round with a scarf, the little cloche coming below her eyes, hair invisible, neck shaved, ochre and carmine on her cheek. 'You're here at last!' It was someone else, very much the same. A second young woman in prescribed form emerging from the abyss, the young man bounded forward a second time towards the cloche, the cheek, the scarf, the stockings—he had to try three young women before he hit—if I may so put it—on the right one. Chastened, he greeted his real young woman with a chill reserve and, while she rebuked him loudly, still a little bemused, he identified her: 'A beauty-spot beneath the eye, right, jade-green earrings and fourteen glass bracelets on the wrist, if I remember rightly.' But at that very moment someone trod on his foot; a female voice emerging from a small cloche hat begged his pardon in the tone of a dry reprimand. He heard the clashing of a dozen or so Czech glass bangles; he spied, along cheeks browner and pinker than natural, two long pendants of imitation jade, and received the tail of a motley scarf in his eye. It was then that the young man became possessed by a transport of fear and anger. He bent forward, bit the beautiful cheek of his over-anonymous young woman, and bore her away, newly branded, like the elect heifer of the herd.

Breasts

How do you like them? Like a pear, a lemon, *à la* Montgolfière, half an apple, or a canteloup? Go on, choose, don't be embarrassed. You thought they didn't exist any longer, that they were all over with, absolutely done for, their name ostracized, their amiable or indiscreet turgescence dead and deflated like gold-beater's skin?

If you spoke of them at all, it was to condemn them as vagaries of the past, a sort of collective hysteria, an epidemic of ages now lost in night, isn't that so? If you don't mind, Madame, let's bring things up to date. They exist, and persist, however criticized and persecuted they may be. There is a dour vitality in those who hope. 'Next year in Jerusalem' murmured others of the oppressed over the centuries. Those I have in mind whisper perhaps: 'Next year, in the corsage. . . .'

Everything is possible, the worst seems probable. Enough of hedging! Admit the truth once and for all: *breasts exist!* There are pear-shaped breasts, breasts like a lemon, half an apple (see above). Anarchy mounts—I wish it merited the title of an up-rising. What, is the breast being refashioned, then? By the emplacement yours have abandoned, I swear it, Madame. You're in a fine fix, as they say. Is there to be news of horrors? There is news. Even better, there are fabrications. Relax, Madame. Let a deep sigh of happiness stir your squared boxer's teats, or your agitated rhetorician's chest, for now you may choose. Little cups in light rubber, painted in natural colours, await you. You hesitate between four or five different types? Bah, you buy them all, for they are all charming. Oh! the modest breasts of former days, the arrogant charms for the white tunic embroidered in mother of pearl, and those two mandarines beneath the Spanish shawl! The technique of using them is as simple as possible. An almost invisible band links the two spurious 'assets' at a proper distance; two other bands, passing under your arms, tie behind your back. Veiled with lace or *crêpe de Chine*, these cups, if empty, conceal the void and, if full, gather and immobilize under their domes the secrets of the overflowing parts. . . .

Are you satisfied, then? No? I see how it is. The result is too perfect. It's true. A kind of neutrality, a deadly serenity, informs the sham breast and this itself arouses suspicion. Wait, Madame, I've not finished being helpful. I offer you . . . take them, these two tulle pockets christened 'hold-alls' by an over-witty woman. 'It's not ill-meant,' she asseverates, 'it just had to be thought of. Nothing can outmanoeuvre my hold-alls. You've too much of *them*, they overflow on all sides? I gather them for you, I centralize them, each in their place, come on now, everything must go back! *Yours* are not wide enough and are too long? I grasp them and knead them for you, I mould them into proper shape—it's only a question of knack—and beneath my tulle, yours can aspire to Venus! Madame has noticed the little hole in the centre to allow the nipple through? That's a mark of genius. That gives life to the whole undertaking!'

I should have wagered, Madame, that I would have overwhelmed you with this stroke. I see you are lukewarm and undecided. Ah! One can't revive a cult at one go, you still reject the twin miracles, so worshipped once. Your nihilism still rests on that unrelenting sentence: 'Nothing too much.' Here we are, at the height of summer. You're leaving for the Normandy seaside, the daily bathe. The women there feel compelled to show themselves brown of limb, flat-bottomed, with no more hip than a bottle of Rhine wine, while the gentlemen are narrow-waisted, laced like Cossacks, and fine-chested. I am inopportune, with my tricks as a precursor of breasts. I need only have first glanced at the new bathing costumes for women, stolen, this year, from the little girls' shelves. Away with yesterday's swimsuit! Or better, hide it, I beg you, under the little checked sleeveless apron that my daughter wore two years ago. Cut at the level of the thigh, the dress of a five-year-old tot in shiny red taffeta with black braid will make the baby happy when mother has given up bathing. Small panels, knots at the back, a six-inch skirt beneath a childish tunic, smocks hitherto reserved for the schoolroom, the elegance of the elementary school, there, that's for Dinard, that's for Deauville! I concede that bathing, breasts, scare you. You are afraid, sheltering them under Claudine's smock, of giving yourself that little 'Chas-Laborde' look that attends every dumpy woman dressed *en gamine*, and you are right. Well then, why not use, between flesh and skin, the supplementary epidermis recently invented, the body-stocking of pure rubber which holds you tighter than a lover from armpit to groin, and even lower. Its hidden strength, uniformly exerted, appears only in use. What matter if it reduces the shape of the female body to the mere contour of a cylinder! Sausage you must be, sausage you shall be. And while a slow strangulation accelerates your heartbeat and congests your cheek you can savour the subtle pleasures of an odoriferous perspiration that gathers the

rubber's sulphurous essence, the human body's acidity. . . . I need
say no more. Adopt this elastic hair-shirt, Madame. You will find
that it serves both vanity and virtue.

Paperweights

This one? Fifteen hundred francs. See, it's signed and dated. . . .

I see. I see that at the centre of the hemispheric paperweight of
thick glass there snuggles a caramel flourish whose section presents
the figure of a star, a rose, a small squirrel, a holothurian, a duck,
or the branched, ramifying hexagon of snow-crystals seen through
a lens. The whole, designed in bold colours, evokes the bottom of
the sea, a garden *à la française*, a jar of Viennese acid-drops, and
costs fifteen hundred francs.

Fifteen hundred francs. I consider the object dispassionately and
compare it with the one I have, which is even more beautiful. In
the days when my very dear Annie de Pène and I used to haunt
the flea-markets, we paid three francs, or a hundred sous, for these
playthings now so sanctified and revalued by fashion. We hid
them, so as to browse in secret on their puerile monstrosity. Annie
had a thing about a paperweight where imprisoned air bubbles
shone like globules of mercury above a drowned pansy.

'But,' she would say mournfully, 'I know that the one with the
forget-me-not and the swallow belongs to a Madame P. . . who
won't sell it, and the very thought of it makes my life miserable!'

She laughed; the laughter lit up a golden fleck in her brown
eyes, the most mischievous, the most penetrating brown eyes that
ever adorned the face of a blonde. Already infatuation was born.
Her more discreet victims concealed it or, taken by surprise, ex-
cused themselves as if for a monomania: 'What d'you expect . . .
it's frightful, this glass object, but it belonged to my great uncle . . .
my mother always had it on her writing-desk. . . .'

Annie de Pène used to prophesy : 'You'll see, they'll get on to them soon enough, these paperweights! Just now, I'm fed up with the chemist in the rue de la Pompe. Only this morning I bought some bicarbonate of soda from him that I didn't need, and some chest liniment that upsets my heart, in the hope that he'd sell me his paperweight with the red rose. Another ten francs thrown away, and for nothing!'

She claimed, rightly, that these glassmakers' masterpieces found shelter with the concierges, and she would suddenly enter a lodge during a walk : 'What floor is Monsieur Defaucomprey? . . . Is Madame Etcheverry on the third floor? . . . The workshops of Messieurs Barnavaux and Coquelourde, please?'

The time it took to put the question and hear the reply was enough for her. Sometimes the darting, brilliant chestnut gaze discovered on the mantelpiece—rounded, bulging, like the luminous cryptogram of the shadow zones—a paperweight. . . . Then Annie, all honey and careful phrases, would start a conversation, praise the baby, stroke the cat, finally approach the paperweight, her imperative desire, in lessening circles. . . . But one day when she asked in a tone of perfect assurance for an improvised 'Monsieur Gaucher' the concierge replied without quitting her armchair : 'There he is now, just on his way down, call him or he'll be through the arch without stopping . . .'

'No, no!' interrupted Annie hastily, 'I only wanted to leave this for him . . . you can give it to him when he gets back. Don't forget, mind!'

She dragged me away, cowardly abandoning a yard and a quarter of excellent suspender elastic that she had just bought.

Well, now they're the rage, these pustulous, incestuous products of the English sweetmeat and the magnifying lens. They've also something of the medusa who perhaps inspired them. Nevertheless, the ladies who currently collect paperweights are well known, Mme Lanvin, Mme Bouniols; Germaine Beaumont and Pierre Battendier shared the rare pieces collected by their mother, Annie de Pène. The Hôtel des Ventes, though it has seen so many others, was in an uproar at the auctions when an unknown collector broke up his collection last year. How long will the new fad last? Longer than one thinks, as it always does when fashion alights on a nobly and entirely useless object. The paperweight now belongs to fine art, just because of its uselessness. It presses no paper, it does not hang from the wall, it cannot be made into a lamp like a vulgar Persian pot, it is not embroidered in cross-stitch like an old print, nor does it cover a lampshade like a precious silk, and no one has ever been heard to suggest that it could be adapted to make a handbag. It evades every degrading usage, the exploiting temper of the modern woman who sacrifices everything to furnish a house and sighs before a slender upright Virgin of the fifteenth century, 'What a marvellous pedestal for a table!' It's not the paperweight that will be turned into a divan or into a 'stylish' telephone apparatus. It can't be cut up into sheets to make a boudoir canopy, like a humble screen from Coromandel. It mocks at the ingenious construction of powder-boxes and shrugs a shoulder, so to speak, at the onyx fashioned into a cigarette-case.

In answer to the uninventive collector who asks herself 'Should it be a god, a table, or a bowl?' it has chosen to be a god. It reigns, no more convex than the forehead of an obstinate spouse, good for nothing, polished, receiving the incense of the faithful. Its crystal soul reveals its every thought, and it thinks little. It is both various and simple, witness of the fervour and the ignorance of those who shaped it. A flower, a little silver sheep, a cactus, a dreamy confusion of sea-creatures, a spreading cross, the emblem of the Legion of Honour . . . that's enough. Our imbecility does the rest. But we must also take into account, to the credit of today's plaything, its shape, so like a sphere, and its thick substance, translucent and distorting. The crystal sphere, an abyss, a snare for images, resort of the weary spirit, source of chimeras, maintains its mysterious attraction for man. When I asked Annie de Pène 'Why do we like these glass balls?' she replied : 'Don't bother me. I know nothing about it. A glass ball, it makes one's mouth water. It's probably a sin.'

Novelties

You take a marabout,* you shave him. And to fill the cup of his ignominy you degrade him, before exposing him for all to see. . . . If these lines chance to be seen by a Moslem it will give him a dreadful shock. To humiliate a saint of Islam thus!

Happily, it's only a matter of fashionable wear. As for degrading the marabout, well and good. Pink or red, violet or blue, he'll be none the uglier for it . . . but shaving him . . . why not shear a chicken or depilate an angora? The rabbit and the marabout, both shorn, are paradoxically allied with that other monstrosity which dishonoured our hats for so long—the glycerined ostrich-feather. (I trust that Joseph Delteil will allow me to dedicate to him, as a delicate offering, these two singularly linked words; I can't forget that he is the author of *The Incestuous Sponge*.)

It is a strange industry that appropriates a downy animal covering—light, warm, smooth to the touch—to destroy it by chemistry or electricity and then to announce 'Behold this unrecognizable skin from which we have removed the living grass and left the stubble! Behold these bound bundles of feathers, with the last of the winged down still adhering! Behold this miserable, nearly bald broom, whose remaining strands have been stuck together by an ingenious treacle! You may wear these remains as proudly as plume or caparison and, what's even more remarkable, no one will laugh!' A fact. It would make me cry rather.

Quick, let's get drunk to forget it. The drunkenness of deliverance, the great wind of change. The little cloche sounds its own knell. Just when one had given up any hope of ever dethroning it, the little concave hat suddenly expires. Its dominion had lasted for more than two lustra. Now, we're told it's done for. By whom? Pah . . . by unimaginative usurpers who mistake eccentricity for courage: the hexagonal skull-cap, the top hat, the pastry-mould,

* *Marabout* can mean either a Moslem holy man or a marabou stork whose feathers were used for decoration.

the inverted bucket, the old-fashioned chamber-pot. Let's put on our heads the truncated bucket which 'gives an Oriental look', the 'amusing' mould, the hexagon said—who'd have thought it—to rejuvenate, the 'stylish' top hat and the 'becoming' chamber-pot— I could give you a thousand examples. Let us savour these ephemeral indulgences whose days are numbered for, in the shadow, there waits and watches, assured of a triumphant return—the little cloche.

Charming extinguisher, friendly shelter for tired eyes, you're on the shelf now. Born of a rudimentary logic, it is the tubular hat just now that crowns the crabbed geometrical masterpiece known as the tube-dress which, like Jeanneton's doll, has neither front nor back. O sadism, O mortification! To inhabit, even if only for a few hours a day, a stove-pipe, the interior of a drain, of a stick of macaroni. The modern woman takes a peculiar delight in this. And whenever fashion reduces the breadth and increases the length of the malleable female body, certain accessories of the toilet become deformed in the opposite direction. Just as the long stalk of the Brussels sprout adorns itself at the right moment with tiers of edible tumours, so the tube-woman hangs from her neck and ears excrescences of hollow silver, notable for their size if not for their weight. Silver was ever a poor, sad metal. Earrings of tarnished silver, tarnished necklaces of silver spheres, take up a lot of room, have little lustre, darken the skin, and anyone but a Negress would disdain them in favour of glassware. These not so brilliant spheres do not even capture the distorted reflection that dances in the centre of the silvered garden globe, their scintillating rival. But they are surprising in their sphericism on a wisp of a woman, flanked in addition by an umbrella. An umbrella? Is that really an umbrella? I quiz the object that Madame Blanche Vogt forgot at my place. She dropped in and I imagined that she had come straight from some Cancale estate by the sea; for she was wearing a dress of light silk, bright red, printed with violet and yellow flowers, shoes of scarlet kid, and flesh-coloured stockings. These maritime appurtenances reached their climax in a little umbrella of bronzed taffeta, a few inches high and broader than it was long, whose handle was decorated with a terrible and probably prehistoric knob; but it was a modern caprice that had carved

in the thickness of its hard wood garlands of little flowers painted
in natural colours.

I haven't yet returned this strange umbrella, this chunky dwarf,
to its owner. I've arranged it beside a carved wooden siren, also
dwarfish, next to a bottle-base in greenish glass picked up on the
beach, polished, mellowed, translucent and turbid as a jelly-fish,
next to two rare shells with pink lips. . . . Strange, my friends
exclaim at sight of the siren, the glass bauble and the shells, but
they have no cry of surprise for the gem of my collection, the
flower-decked truncheon skirted with cockchafer taffeta—in fact,
the umbrella.

I meant to tell the ottoman, an old flame that returns, newly
done up, from afar, what I thought of it in two words; two words
touching on its ill-humour in enveloping us, its misplaced gravity,
its temper that takes offence at a drop of rain. But here I am side-
tracked by a musical reverie. The king of weavers doesn't stop at
inventing materials, he also invents their names. Hardy neologisms,
sounds of arabesque richness, calm as Tibetan wool, you caress the
ear with a harmony that derives from savage chant and waggish
invention. It's not for you I speak, kasha, cat-named kasha :

'On your ravishing breast that your modesty concealed*
Crosses and recrosses in beauty a scarf of kasha !'

But, when I read the roll of crepellaine, bigarella, poplaclan, of
djirsirisa and gousellaine—I forget how many !—I am seized by
a phonetic rapture and begin to think in pure poplacote dialect.
Allow me, in taking leave of you, dear reader, to glove myself with
filavella, to put my rubespadrillavellaines on my feet, to wear my
djissatutbanecla hat; now's the time, at low tide to go fishing
among the anfractuosities of rockaskaia, congrepellina and the
zibeline sea-bream.

* *Cacha.*

Late Season

Winter approaches. A bold statement that dates from a few weeks ago and in particular from the day when I saw the first chestnut-seller install herself beneath the massive arcade of the porte Saint-Vincent. Before her, English elegance, conquering the heights of Saint-Malo, had heralded frost. Fashionable London of Saint-Malo does not shrink before the audacious innovations that astound the eye and capture the soul of the artist. No doubt of it, it must have been admiration that held me captive at sight of a young Islander, serene despite the shower, beneath a cape of black marocain with monkey collar. Some artifice of fashion simulated, at shoulder-level and on the lower part of the cape, the greenish plaques that grease imprints on any black material. Under the cape could be glimpsed a ravishing shirt-dress in braided cotton, in old rose turning to yellow. And the fringe of black fur that hemmed the bottom of the garment was not so long that one could not see, as coquettish as unexpected, two bare feet shod in espa-drilles very cunningly decolourized by one of those techniques of which shoemakers of genius guard the secret. And what to say of the hat, of mauve national material and Scottish ribbon? How to praise the handbag-reticule in brushed painted leather, the neck-lace of green bobbles encircling a lorgnette?

Mindful of this dazzling memory, I sought in vain for an anal-ogous ensemble in the great collections, where there was neverthe-less a surprise in store for me.

'Is it you?' I asked Lucien Lelong, 'who is launching the dress in braided pink cotton, covered by a marocain cape . . . ?'

Before I had finished my sentence the young and ebullient *couturier* had evaded me, crying: 'Mme de X's *culotte*, now! What, it's not ready? It only needed gathering at the bottom and fixing two pieces of suède on the. . . .' The rest was lost in the clatter of doors. The door of a delicate lacquer salon opened and there emerged a thin acid voice: 'No, Madame Jeanne, no revolver-pocket. And the base of the jacket to reach the level of the trousers, not an inch more !'

The word 'ski' issuing from invisible lips enlightened me just as I trembled to see myself, to keep up with everyone else, condemned to the smoking-jacket and to the horrible so-called fancy trousers which contract with the jacket an indissoluble union devoid of love or reason.

Winter sports, I've more to say to you. From December to February you nibble at the female skirt, subject to wave and sun from July to September. You have a place in the year determined by the snow-bearing east wind, the west wind that melts the glaciers. But you have for accomplices the hunting season, sea-bathing, African exploration, riding, which—like you—strip Woman of her ancient shackle, the dress. Nowadays every season tolerates and favours the trousered woman, and the *couturier*, endowed with a hound's nose, changes into breeches-maker, knitter, military tailor, rather than lose half his profits. He profits from the woman's boyish infatuation and, cutting his losses, more or less does away with the now useless transitional costume, mid-way between the morning's sportive leggings and the soft draperies of evening. The 'good, safe dress' has had its day. But the Saumur breeches for ladies prosper, and the *lamé* also.

Gold *lamé*, silver *lamé*, copper, steel—they are alike in their rustle, always a little like chocolate wrappings, in their grating chill and in their smell. The enduring vogue for *lamé* indicates the grossness of the female senses, particularly the sense of smell. For the scent of a *lamé* dress, dampened in the course of a warm evening, oxidized while dancing, surpasses in acridity the strong aroma of a removal-man in full activity. It smells of ill-kept silverware, of old copper coins, the brass-cloth; its silken texture does nothing to attenuate the odours that impregnate it; on the contrary.

The other day a slender friend—all my friends are slender—was amusing herself at her *couturier's* trying on some evening dresses she coveted. 'I'm a small 42 !' she announced at every opportunity. Like a stickleback with its nest, she agilely traversed those narrow drainpipes that are labelled, according to their material, as a morning walking-dress or a ball-dress; she went in head first, made her exit with her feet, danced a peacock step before the mirrors, mimed fashionably the amiable scoliosis that was already in vogue in Albert Dürer's time, and steamed, I swear, like a little horse at dressage. A dress of gold and steel *lamé* on a green foundation attracted her, not so much, however, as another of silver *lamé* on black; but then there appeared a copper *lamé* on brown which, as my friend vividly expressed it, 'knocked the rest into a cocked hat' and yet was dethroned by a silver and gold *lamé* on pale pink. Privately, I criticized the irritating uniformity of their design : a metal tube, quite straight, based on a foundation of material. One particular dress, slit from top to bottom, revealed an under-layer of green crêpe and the saleswoman, reassuring my perplexed friend, informed her that 'many of these ladies wore the split sometimes in front and sometimes behind'. She added, mysteriously, that the coming winter would see an 'even more practical' evening gown, thanks to two laterally placed openings above the hem : 'You turn your dress upside-down, you put your arms through the openings and the result is that the embroidery or the material is now on top and looks quite different. What do you think of that, ladies?'

My slender friend did not reply immediately, reduced as she was to the condition of a hermit crab inserted into an unyielding casing, arms raised and blindly beating the air above her invisible head. I felt that I ought to fill in the moments when, as they say in the theatre, people dry : 'I think,' I suggested humorously, 'that it might be simpler perhaps to teach your clients to walk on their hands. . . .'

An angry look reminded me, too late, that nothing is to be gained by being facetious at the expense of taxi-drivers and dressmakers : 'In France, only those who sell Christmas cards and mah-jong sets need bother about English habits. As for walking on hands, we may leave that to the Duchess of Sutherland, who, so it seems, can outclass anyone.'

Furs

She has a car, but she has not got a pearl necklace.

I have, you have, we have a pearl necklace, but they have, will have, might have had a fur-coat.

The car of my cousin is smaller than the pearl necklace of my aunt.

If your grandmother had had a pearl necklace, your mother could have bought a fur coat and sold her car. . . .

In a year or two it will be obligatory; meanwhile the use of the little manual of conversation and syntax from which I quote is optional. In all, it contains three hundred phrases constructed by felicitous combinations of the words 'car', 'pearl necklace' and 'fur coat', with nouns of the second order such as *château, Deauville, aeroplane, blackmail, carat, suicide, concealment of capital,* etc., and thereby capable of universal application. I am told that a *de luxe* edition contains a list of famous necklaces, furs and cars. This list, kept carefully up to date, makes it possible to state that a pearl necklace and a motor-car are interchangeable in precisely opposite directions, but that a fur, if it is not definitely associated with its owner, disappears without trace like a spring soaked up by desert sands.

Certain young women—a woman who possesses everything is inevitably young—own necklace, car and fur together. Instead of remaining in stagnant serenity they relinquish the cares of necklace and car to devote themselves to a prudently graduated collection of fur coats. Hierarchically, the coat progresses from mink to sable, by way of chinchilla.

I knew an artiste—an artiste of the woman-of-the-world type, that is, the minimum of charm with the minimum of talent—who, between a peerless mink and a pedigree sable, lacked the gradation of chinchilla. She retained a constant bitterness because of this and the smile of a woman who has lost an incisor tooth. Another artiste, young and charming, finds herself at present within reach,

if I may so put it, of a sable coat, the waiting, the passionate quest
for which, produce in her the physical trepidation, the dancing
from one foot to the other, that can be seen in children tormented
by a long withheld desire. She has got to ill-treating her last year's
chinchilla and to mishandling and treating—I swear it!—as a
'little tart's fur' her own two-year-old mink which she accuses of
having turned red. . . .

'Master' furrier, since that's how you christen yourself, you can
count on thousands of slaves. You know that furs and roles have
changed, and you are no longer to be heard saying to a customer,
as you bow her over the threshold, 'Your servant, Madame'.
Debt-ridden, the customer bows a shoulder under the hand of
your smart purveyor, male or female, and knows the cost of the
'Goodbye, little one!' that you throw her from the top of the
stairs. She hasn't stolen it, Our Lord furrier. Remind her, whenever necessary, that she is the humiliated descendant of those
women who waited, shivering in the dark of a cave, for a male to
throw some still-bleeding pelt round her nakedness. You won't
need to remind her of the surrender with which the prehistoric
little woman had to pay for the animal's skin.

'For that's one of the things a woman doesn't forget. . . .'

But you care little, furrier, for this voluptuous kind of trifle.
You invent, and how! Never were there fewer furry animals, or
more skins. Rabbit, treated in a hundred ways, has not said its
last word. It was merely an impalpable snow falling from your
hands on the skin of the rat that promoted it to the inaccessible
chinchilla; now you have to marry the wild beast and its victim
and you offer us, as serious as a Batignolles trapper, 'gazelle,
panther-style'. Hybrids that embellish the sordid dialogue of saleswoman and client, while the smallest purchase of a little skin confounds natural history. It was an honest dealer in skins at Toulouse
who boasted to me of the beauty of a large width of burnduck:
'Look, Madame, see how the colour is the same from one end of
the skin to the other. It's very fine burnduck.'

'Is it natural?'

'Oh, Madame, you can't mean it! Real burnduck isn't strong;
this is made from little shaved mink. If you prefer this panther for
the fine facings and bottom of a coat, you'll be pleased with it; we

aren't like those people who make their panther out of good-for-nothing gazelle, I can guarantee it !'

'Really ?'

'As per invoice, Madame! All our panther is made from real kid.'

Amateurs

Sanctifying and extending a privilege hitherto reserved for MM. Sacha Guitry, Fauchois and Verneuil, the Casino of Monte Carlo this year launches the author-actor. Down with the professional! After all, what does the public expect from a lead player bearing a famous name? Talent, emotion, admirable self-control and the clarity of diction acquired through much labour? It's not much. It's monotonous. 'Let us then,' says the Casino Theatre, 'engage the authors themselves and let them loose in their own works. We don't yet know what the public will make of it, but real actors will doubtless experience a moment of gaiety at this novel spectacle and, frankly, it really is their turn. This kind of theatrical gala will at once combine a childlike improvisation and a delightful inexperience.' In which belief the Casino Theatre engaged Tristan Bernard, Jean Sarment, Jacques Deval, hinted at Maurice Rostand, co-opted Léopold Marchand and Colette. Then it sat down, this Casino Theatre, on its ample white backside, rubbed its hands in anticipation, and watched the antics of its squad of author-interpreters while waiting for the moment to laugh. . . .

It's still waiting. Beside the blue sea it dreams of this use of dramatist-interpreter, to which its authority as Monaco's Casino Theatre shall have accorded official acknowledgment and existence, of this amateurism, if I may so describe it, which only asks to become professional. Where now is the promised farce? Where now the light-hearted improvisation, the studio absurdity? Why, here are authors who rehearse as if they hadn't other fish to fry, who know how to walk on to the stage without catching their feet in the carpet, who make up like English ballerinas, take their time and give the audience the glad eye! We have here outsiders who don't fuss about working continuously through the day and half the night, who don't blink before the footlights and who travel with their bottle of gargle! But it's a betrayal! It's not funny any more at all!

My dear Casino Theatre, don't lose heart. It's much funnier even than you think—first for us, the outsiders, who engage ourselves to present our own texts to the public, here one day and there another, and who amuse ourselves to distraction. Maybe Jean Sarment does not share my opinion, but that's because Jean Sarment, a born actor, an author born and bred, no longer has a hobby-horse to ride to death. Ask our natural Tristan if, more than anything, he doesn't like to play in comedy? Ask Jacques Deval if he didn't experience the keenest and most reprehensible pleasure during the time when I had him rehearse the part of Chéri? If you should catch my collaborator Léopold Marchand before his mirror, his face coated with make-up, then, driven by exaggerated professional motivation, he will alter his boxer's face and change in turn into an aged general, a bistro waiter, a Red Indian, a leper and an Indian fakir! There shine in him the dazzling qualities of the amateur interpreter of the first rank— and I don't say this just because Léopold Marchand measures over six feet—the same qualities that dignify Jacques Deval. Jacques Deval counted the lines of the part I offered him and grimaced: 'In my own piece,' he said nonchalantly, 'I'd have ten times as much to spout. . . .' So he turned down the part of Desmond in *Chéri*. Léopold Marchand did not dare to imitate him but cast a grim eye at the excellent Basseuil, a professional, who inherited a more important part in the same piece. And he attempted to console himself by purchasing, for a ten-minute appearance on the stage, a fifty-louis suit as well as a pair of boxing-gloves for seventy francs, special shoes, an English sweater that cost several pounds sterling, and a mauve check cap that made me smile. . . . But one cannot criticize the born amateur with impunity: 'Do I criticize you,' he said acidly, 'for your three

Lelong dresses? Three dresses for three appearances, one for each act!' Masculine surliness will resort to the lowest arguments. What's the point of arguing?

All the same, it's still the case that the company of author-actors 'sets the fashion' as they say. It will last . . . as long as a fashion? There are some very enduring fashions, such as the shirt-dress. . . .

Before me the sea is a fierce blue, the palm-trees a vivid green against a backdrop of advertising bill-boards. But the violets smell of violets and the Italian grape, Madeira-coloured, is within reach of every purse. I might easily forget my dignity as author-interpreter if the furtive yet gigantic shadow of my collaborator did not momentarily block the square as he leaves a perfumer's shop where, I dare say, he has acquired some stick of make-up that was missing from his amateur's collection. Punctually, and with papal severity, we shall both be ready in advance in our artistes' box this evening, like the brave amateurs we are. The producer has no worries so far as we are concerned. Forgotten are the anxieties evoked last week by Tristan Bernard, when he disappeared to go gambling between two appearances in his role. . . .

Dear Tristan, whatever you do, you'll never be an amateur!

Empty Pockets

Well, that's that. We've done the rounds but we admit that we're flat out. Exhausted, drained, here we are seated on a modern cushion given us too late to be sent, a rose pinned to its bulging *lamé* belly, to a friend. From now on, terrified, we watch the approach of Easter, hatching its eggs. . . .

The children have been stuffed. Nauseated with sweets, cinema and circus, they are back at their hygienic school, where they will be restored to health. Among themselves they speak less of their

own presents than of the ones their parents have received. 'My
papa has a new six-cylinder . . .' 'And what d'you think, when
Mama opened her jewel-case . . .' They are the children of today,
greedy, impatient. They accept the cinema while waiting to travel,
the mechanical toy while anticipating a motor-car. My daughter,
aged eleven and a half, announces the make of every car as it
speeds by, and she is always right. She calculates under her breath
and asks : 'How many years' ordinary New Year's presents would
it take to make a five horse-power?' The poor child doesn't realize
that ordinary New Year's presents don't exist any more. December
has brought chestnuts at twenty francs a pound, roses at eight
francs apiece, truffles at a hundred francs the kilo. The little
Pont-aux-Choux soup-tureen was marked up at a thousand francs
in the window on New Year's Eve; it will be less in January, but
we shan't have any money left to buy it.

January, month of empty pockets ! The snow of the mountain-
tops calls us, but everything has to be paid for and snow is as
expensive as white marabout. What woman would dare tread it
without having refitted herself with Saumur breeches, double and
triple stockings, nailed boots, sweaters, fur coat, scarves, eider-
down-gloves? The tourist is ruined by his equipment before even
reaching the mountain-slope; what use will they be, those deep,
buttoned, leather-lined pockets? Let us endure this evil month,
anxious as a theatrical producer's forehead. With a diver's courage
more than one woman this month plunges into some neglected
chest, into wardrobes given over to darkness and camphor. The
purse may be empty but one must nevertheless keep up with the
spring fashions, though the holidays have put a large part of the
wardrobe out of action. The pearled tunic, fatigued by dancing,
is on its way out; indoor fireworks and pudding-sauce have aged
the velvet sheath-dress by a year; and this obstinate rain can't
have been helpful to the hygiene of the afternoon dress in crêpe
marocain.

'We must see about it,' say the women. They see about it.
Between January and March, Madame, you will meet your newly
adorned friends and you will cry out in admiration, but with a
desperation in your praises that demands an explanation : 'This?'
your friend will say. 'But this is my three-piece from X. . . . Look,

it's fifteen months old, my dear, and I'm not ashamed of it!' This is uttered in a frank, honest, high voice that adds, more gently and offhandedly: 'Have you noticed that the new collections have gone back to exactly the same details in the neck and shirt material? It's very strange.'

Empty pockets, high hearts—this is the month for grand feminine resignation. My friend Valentine exhibits, in January, the embarrassment of a peahen at moulting-time. Each New Year, like an equinoctial tide, brings her its unvarying manifestations of economy. The week of Twelfth Night, she nibbled her piece of flan at my place and the *vin de paille* loosened her tongue—a result that might have been brought about just as well by a glass of water.

'It's all over,' she tells me. 'I give up.'

It crossed my mind that she might be taking the veil: still, I made inquiry.

'What? Why, the *couturiers*, of course! Thank heavens! And I've no regrets, understand? I've just discovered an absolute treasure . . . a little dressmaker, my dear, who for two hundred and fifty francs can make me exactly the same dresses that I pay —used to pay, it's all over now!—eighteen hundred to three thousand francs for at X. . . .'

'No! Is that possible?'

'Absolutely, I tell you. It's better finished, even, than at X. . . because X. . . has too many customers and he botches things. So you see, for the price of one dress from X. . . I've just ordered eleven dresses. It's not worth going without! Real pleasure, real smartness, lie in variety, believe me!'

I congratulated my friend Valentine. She seemed so happy that I did not remind her of her avowal of Twelfth Night, 1924, an avowal during which I learned that, tired of modest and ineffectual dresses, she was leaving her jobbing dressmaker to become a client of the famous X. . . .

'You understand, it's all over. I shan't be taken in by those little dressmakers any more. Thank heavens! There are ten dresses, my dear, ten dresses I'm giving up quite new. Money thrown away, bad temper, four thousand francs in the gutter, that's what comes of trying that little dressmaker! Now, at X. . .'s I get for my four thousand francs two marvellous dresses which won't lose their shape and won't go out of fashion, that I can always wear happily. To be really smart doesn't mean having a lot of dresses; on the contrary, it's wearing the indisputable style of a great house.'

Silks

From obscure depths, where sometimes glides the slow reflection that illumines abundant lazy springs, there rises an enormous umbel, a kind of star. Its dome, flush with the surface of the water, bears the colours of the fiery begonia, the full-red rose, its drowned edges descend to the red of hot metal, of pomegranate stained purple by shadow. Behind the empurpled floating creature sways a trailing branch, fronded, of algal-green. . . .

However, we are only talking of velvet, and a printed flower. The creator of the design declares : 'That's a poppy . . .' and so he believes. But I know full well that his flower—bulbous, umbilicated, delicately segmented, fringed, and trailing a filamentous train—is a jelly-fish. If I tell the designer that it's a jelly-fish he will protest with the haughty manner of a misunderstood artist. The primordial sea is a long way off. The monster or the flower it engenders in our minds emerges, as does the fruit of the water-chestnut, at the end of a stalk so long that we give no thought to its submerged root. But the beauty of the material displayed reveals the secret of inspiration : at the heart of richly moiré velvet, touched by the watery sheen that plays on a light-absorbing surface, the poppy has become a jelly-fish.

I touch, I contemplate these modern silks, the most costly of feminine adornments. Sure of his supremacy, proud of his magical workings, he that weaves them says gently : 'I am supreme.' What point in modesty here? All is magnificence, inflated even more this year by certain monstrous features. Consider this giant gloxinia, that gapes like a little maelstrom at the corner of a great

square of silk! The edges of its mouth are tinted the colours of
the rainbow, as happens with cataclysmic phenomena. It is as
beautiful as a rainbow, as the eye of an octopus.

On an implacable background of gold there turn and climb long,
black, half-open pods whose stalks are daughters of the noxious
viburnum and the snake. Applied to the flat hip of the nymph of
1925, they will incline her towards evil spells, no less than these
lanceolate flames, a fire that is not quenched, purple, green, sun-
yellow, that thrust their several tongues towards a bare throat.

What gold, silver and red copper, mixed with the silk! Over
the material designed for artificial light there reign the splendour
and brutality always imposed by epochs when fashion suffers
from poverty of form. The little rectangular tunic goes back to,
recovers, the luxury of Byzantine gowns. When the designer sleeps
the weaver wakes and works miracles. Using more or less torsion
he curbs or cossets the brilliance of the metal thread, evokes a
background, interposes between design and spectator a mist of
illusion. One piece of illusion detains me for a long time as I seek
mechanically with my finger to judge the exact distance of this
floating spider's web in pure silver, here concave, convex there,
that separates me from a curtain of half-seen roses—yellow, red,
pink, against a distant black sky. . . . It's clear that a certain kind
of phantasmagoria is popular here, an optical deception that is
akin to wit. Avenues of enormous, multicoloured lozenges affront
the eye, then recede with the vertiginous diminution of nocturnal
reflections. A play of lines plots deceptive perspectives on an art-
less crêpe, while on another crêpe the eye takes in, from bird's eye
or aeroplane height, tree-top after tree-top, crinkled foliage em-
phasized by a little stroke of vivid lightning-blue.

There is no pleasure without fatigue and that of the eye, if it is
prolonged, is particularly dispiriting. Too much gold, gold embroidery on a gold background, too much light and line, too much
damascened lampas, eventually engender the lassitude caused by
overrich museums. Yet our satiety is deferred by an artistic device
not at once apparent, that consists of using an invisible grey, if I
may so put it, applied to the reverse of a leaf, an ardent petal,
insinuated between two red gleams, between two segments of
green. A grey that caulks and stops the fissures where colours fly

together, a concentric grey like the zone of feeble reflection that bounds a breach in smooth water.

Let us take our ease in those gardens which, flowering this winter, await the sun and the women of the summer to come. The rose abounds there, a rose faithful to the pictorial tradition our mothers cherished around 1880. Such material is decorated with veritable floral 'portraits', portraits of rich, rather heavy, well-fleshed roses of scrupulous accuracy. Farewell to the 'stylized' eye-shaped rose, farewell to the rose shaped like a snail! The roses I brush against bathe in a light mist, in an air atremble with heat, and I think of those miraculous machines whose steel finger, applying a mother-of-pearl hue here, a splash of light or the green mirror of a moist leaf there, never errs. . . .

Other roses are strewn on other silks, in rustic and ruinous taste; there is the rose borrowed from Persia, the rose of carpets, flat, crushed, laid out to be grateful to the bare foot. The gentle orange seeks the company of the bright rose and the mauves of the sweet-pea are enhanced by a shadowed white ground, mysteriously besmirched. But the dishevelled poppy needs no contrivance. Its torch flames out against the white, against the raw green of the young corn, and burns with such fierceness that women may well be afraid of it, come summer.

But they won't be frightened so easily. Come summer, they will go away, a grass-green skirt round their loins, a red poppy at their breast, fork-tongued lilies at their heart's height. The master of these gardens of fabrics tells me how readily his guests become infatuated, feverishly plunging their bare arms into the murmuring waves of silk. But they are not overawed and, the first ecstasy over, unastonished, they seek a star to garner for their corsage, a meteor to plant in their shorn hair. . . . Whosoever weaves the moon, the sun and the blue shafts of the rain, knows that neither prodigality nor splendour exhausts the depths of feminine avidity. So he restorts to certain perversities.

This year he has been cloistered with a choice bundle of priceless skeins spun by silkworms, murmurs an incantation, baptizes the web with a talismanic elixir, and brings to light amid cries of astonishment . . . the most perfect imitation of a little hound's tooth woollen, at twelve ninety-five the metre!

The author in her dressing-room

Collette around 1910

Logic

Bravo, bravo! They've made up their minds, most of them. The dark days of February, crabbed icy March, April of the two faces —one violet with cold, the other warmly pink—have seen them clothed in yellow oilskins, greenish gaberdines, topped with a little hat glistening with water, minus umbrella and hands in pockets. Bravo! They've braved the vertical rain, the slanting wind, the horizontal snow that adhered to the eyelashes. There they are, the practical women, the pioneers of 1925, good managers today, tomorrow's voters, those who . . .

. . . Those, O Dithyrambic, who have paraded their old and new virtues all winter, at zero temperature and below, on two soles no thicker than a finger-nail, fastened by three little patent-leather straps across a flesh-pink silk stocking. And don't try to tell me about the mottled or ribbed stocking they tried to popularize this year! It was admirable, the ribbed stocking, on the avenue du Bois in the mornings, I mean between twelve and one. It attracted attention, produced as it was in five or six versions. But all winter, in the puddles, spattered with mud, blemished, pitiful, grotesque, indecorous, you must admit one has seen only the pink silk stocking and those wretched little slippers. Oilskins, gaberdines, lynx and beaver collars, topcoats of panther-cum-mole and jaguar-cum-kid, yes, yes, women have pampered their bodies, sheathed in all the necessary fur and quilting, but their care, their coquettish and hygienic ingenuity, has not reached below the knees. Why? Enthusiast, give me a reason. The vagaries of Fashion have a goal and often make sacrifice to aesthetics. But this! And the bare-fleshed stocking beneath the tailored costume! And this poverty of the leg, its cold hue emerging from a rain-proof! And the defenceless foot, sullied by a shower, preposterous under a fur hem as big as a child's body! And the attitude, either shivering or cynical, of a woman seated in a drawing-room, seated on the banquette of a bus! And the unfinished appearance, so

J.F.M.—D

oddly scamped, got up in a hurry, imparted to a town outfit by
two legs clothed as for an evening's frolics!

Having decided to shorten skirts still further, to lead women
towards the 'seven-year-old look' (and five francs extra by age, as
the catalogues say), Fashion hesitates, not daring to risk, at least
in town, the Asiatic trousers that are the unique resort of modesty
and hygiene. I should add 'of common sense', since it would
enforce some concealment in the great lump of a woman, rare
surviving instance of the extinct chubby genus, in the sylph
mounted on stilts, neither of whom hesitates to exhibit, beneath
the pearly mesh of a '44, fine', twenty inches of legs fit to offend
the good Lord—and even his creature.

No, Enthusiast, no, out-and-out Feminist, don't try to make me
share your lyricism and don't expect me to foresee any good from
a female legislator who is incapable of a warm-foot policy, from a
female deputy who, with fingers numb from cold and stamping
her feet, winds up a session in somewhat cavalier style to run to
the hearth and the radiator.

All very well if, hardened, women become used to trampling
the brown slush, the transient whiteness of the snow, with an
invulnerable foot! But hardly so. There have been nothing but
complaints all winter and our barefooted wanderers danced with
the cold from one foot to the other like a cat on hot bricks. Haven't
you heard them, in a restaurant: 'Quick, *maître d'hôtel*, a hot-
water bottle, a brick! I can't feel my feet any longer. Oh, my
dear, this cold! I've been unable to keep my poor feet warm all
day and I know I'm going to have a red nose this evening! ... My
dear, just believe me, the skin of my thighs is all chapped because
of these very short dresses. . . .'

All the same, Enthusiast, do not look down your long nose.
Think of the good weather ahead, the warmth, of the thin winter
sandal at last yielding place to the thick golf shoe, to the rubber-
soled shoe, of the female foot, in July, simmering to boiling-point
on odorous rubber and chrome leather. Amuse yourself, already
resolved to applaud them, in enumerating the small inventions we
owe to elegance. Celebrate here and now the return of the dress-
necks that reach up to the ears, the sleeve that lengthens with the
summer and shortens in winter. Sing the great knot tied under

the chin, the three turns of muslin, the Royer-Collard lapels, the enormous boa in cock-feathers reserved for the dog-days, and sing also, while you're at it, the suppression of our hat-brims. Come the fine weather, for us the nose that peels and the eye that waters in the powerful light!

Logic, feminine logic, astounding decisions, sudden, possibly long-meditated changes, secrets of little boyish heads, arrogant above sheaths of gold and pearls. . . . At the *couturier's* a Byzantine splendour promenades on shorn collegians. Lelong drapes ravishing little emperors of the decadence, sexless types accomplished in grace, so young and so ambiguous that I could not refrain from suggesting to the young *couturier*, on a day of upheaval in his court of models : 'Why don't you employ—oh, quite innocently—some adolescent boys? The lively shoulder, the well-poised neck, the long leg, the absent breast and hip, there are plenty who'd give good value . . .'

'I understand perfectly,' interrupted the young master *couturier*. 'But the boys who get used to dresses very soon acquire a gait, an exaggerated feminine grace in comparison with which my young female models, I assure you, would come to resemble transvestites.'

Everyday Adventures

For me, there are no theatrical recollections to evoke Duse, who died this week. Twice, in Rome during the war, the cinema offered her for my delectation. On the first occasion she was playing in the film the part of an aged peasant woman. Beneath the knotted shawl, beneath the calico and the dark apron, she displayed hair of a luminous whiteness, an erect, firm body, and eloquent hands capable of saying everything that a somewhat constrained, even intimidated, countenance refused the screen. During her great scene these hands, lifted towards a high window, called to a much-loved child. La Duse turned her back to the audience, which saw only the calico blouse, the kerchief tied over her hair, and the hands at the ends of outstretched arms, such hands—loving, beating wings, extended and elevated by their shadow to the very edge of the window—that, at that moment, sobs and sighs escaped the sensitive Italian crowd with which I mingled.

On the second occasion, a few days later, I had sought in another dark, cool cinema some shelter from the Roman spring, exploding everywhere in wistaria, irises, lilac, and so fiery that even the *ponentino* brought no relief. A friend said to me very quietly : 'Behind us, that woman in black, that's Eleanora Duse.' I recognized the luminous hair, swept up in a slanting flame above the brow, restrained by a black hat, and the large, deep eye-sockets, where the eyes swam in a shade that enhanced their brilliance. Only the small nose remained the nose of a young woman, a demanding ironic nose, a nose prompt to anger and disdain.

This famous face, turning to right and left, followed the episodes of a wretchedly dramatic film and there could be read in its every feature a great and tender simplicity, without trace of suspicion. But the interval, bringing back the light, also brought a good many admirers around La Duse. She received their homage standing and shook a number of hands. She did not smile, held her face rather defensively, and the little nose, offended, quivered with disdain.

'See,' whispered my enthused Italian companion, 'see what a great lady she is!'

I have never witnessed such hauteur, doubtless involuntary, in Sarah Bernhardt, who blossomed in the love of the crowd, the unknown, the passer-by, and who gave a smile in return for the thrown flower, a kiss or a salutation launched in the air.

When I chanced to be a passing guest at her table, four or five months before her death, Sarah's youth and octogenarian coquetry almost left me speechless, and I was all eyes and ears for her vigilant chatter, her pale, exalted gaze, her hands—agile ossicles playing beneath a skin as delicate as the new skin of healed burns. She poured boiling water on measured doses of powdered coffee, filled the cups herself, while asking my opinion—for the malicious pleasure of voicing her own—of those who, stumbling in her footsteps, assumed the roles she had created. What desire to please, what near-posthumous effort still to shine! What determination to forget, to make others forget, the present physical decay and to reconstruct for us, by a single movement of the eyelids, drawn up to the summit of the forehead, by an imperious rap on the table with her dry, resonant fingers, by a fugitive, evanescent smile, the Sarah of former days, the eternal Sarah!

They were not fond of each other, these two dead women. They are at rest, having neither known nor wished for rest during their lives. Perhaps, in some unknown place, they pine and complain, La Duse that she can no longer, on the stage, weep the tears of a woman in love and betrayed, Sarah that she has ceased to simulate so marvellously the feminine suffering against which the theatre rendered her immune.

Did they suffer in growing old? Not for long. La Duse respected the wrinkles on her face, though there was as much negligence as dignity to be divined in her scruples. Sarah attained old age without feeling it, but she touched up her features with colour and make-up with an Oriental and intelligent taste for adornment. La Duse, because she had loved and never got over it, kept the same open wound in her bosom; Sarah, cradled and sustained by the fanatic adoration of the crowd, never weakened on her single leg. . . . After them, who no longer counted the years, survivors plan to count the days and hours, to mortify themselves and keep on guard. For our age has witnessed the flowering of a rather disturbed and rather self-ashamed style on stage and screen and in literature : first there is the adolescent starlet, the film heroes haven't always reached the age of matriculation, and out of twenty new novels half relate, minutely and gloatingly, the first giddiness of youth. It takes a hundred and fifty pages to prepare their fall, the rest is rushed through in forty pages—the rest being love. The Daphnis and Chloë of today, seeing themselves in the stream, sigh : 'When we were young. . . .' I know a little girl of eleven who takes stock of herself in the mirror and grimaces : 'I tell you, Mama, that dressmaker makes me look old !' Another, at twelve, acts bewildered to rejuvenate herself : 'What a child I am !' No gain for candour here; on the contrary. Was it with great smiles, limpid by artifice, that they won and betrayed the confidence of trusting parents, all those little 'lost girls' who went off furnished only with a school satchel or a carton of milk? Sometimes one is brought back and then silence closes over her, after the grand inquest in the newspapers and the maternal lamentations. 'It is thought that some shady individual tempted little Suzanne away . . . smothered her cries. . . .' But no. This simple, crude and tragic picture is not—as one learned too late—the truth. Little Suzanne, little Eugénie, in fact the little girl, too little, is a child of our time, matured in the light of images, the dazzle of arc-lights, the batteries of looks, the sound of words, as out of season as a first fruit. With the adventurous brow of the ignorant, with a chill and foolish bumptiousness, the diplomacy of prisoners, it is she who walked deliberately into a trap as a stream yawns open into an azure gulf, it is she who negotiated with the man lying in wait. Every child is unfathomable. But what to think of the vanished little girl who, brought back, restored to her family, goes out again, melts at night like a cat between door-jamb and half-open door? We, who are only simple adults, we dare not think of the little girl who, without a quiver, puts her hand into the hand held out from the shadow, the hand that perhaps will close on the childish neck to leave a collar of hollowed imprints, the colour of violets. . . .

One mustn't shiver overmuch, condemn too eagerly. Lyricism and tragedy express themselves as best they may in everyday life; a predestined child will employ new methods to distress her family, that is, to try to be grown-up. The generation that engendered two famous tragediennes still streamed with romantic tears. Which of our mothers would enjoy the fevered, ambitious adolescence, obsessed with stanzas, of a Duse or a Sarah? Yet our own reticent and stolid children nurse the same disease, the same promise, for all escape is lyricism and conforms to what Hélène Picard has called 'Poetry, the one great sin. . . .'

Assassins

Stimulated by a facile press, the curiosity of the crowd extends to the four lunatics painted by Géricault. They are five portraits, precise and devoid of mystery. It is rather odd that there is less secrecy and horror in these madmen's faces than, for instance, in the study of avulsed, mixed-up limbs enhanced by a small strip of linen and a little pale blood, or in the enchanting head, with eyelids invaded by shadow, of the *Dead Young Man with Closed Eyes*. But I note, looking more closely at *The Mad Assassin*, a detached expression, eyebrows raised in vaguely injured astonishment, a kind of haughty indifference, that I am not seeing for the first time. If I ignore the madman's inflamed complexion and twisted mouth, the rest of the face reminds me of Landru, whom I studied throughout a long hearing. This well-mannered man suffered a most tumultuous session that day. The subtle attorney-general and Moro-Giafferi, carried away in a wild delirium, abounded with threats, venomous allusions and shouting, and the flutter of their sleeves ventilated the chamber. The public, sympathetically excited, showed an equal abandon and the sound of their voices re-echoed. Above the uproar, Landru, with a uniform monochrome pallor, preserved a silence that expressed an opinion. His rare responses were uttered in an agreeable tone of voice. On two occasions only, during a period of four hours, he turned to-

wards the over-excited public and his gaze wandered without
insistence, dark under astonished eyebrows, showing towards all of
us a barely perceptible censure. All around him there was talk of
flaying, bones and burning; a surviving fiancée came to the bar
but met with small success there, suddenly intimidated, once more
submissive to the calm, dark, unfathomable eye that neither sought
nor avoided her, brilliant as a bird's eye and, like a bird's, devoid
of language, tenderness and melancholy. An eye created to see, to
spy, to diminish, to conceal emotion, to weigh up every passer-by
and every spectacle. An eye as serene as that of the first men, an
eye that contemplated the shed blood, death and pain without
blinking a lid—as very small children do, as our ancestors did
before they had invented pusillanimity, when they still enjoyed
the blood freed from its fleshly prison, the water springing out of
the ground, milk spurting from the udder and the juice of crushed
grapes. This beautiful, inexorable eye did, however, as I watched
it, settle on the blonde plaits and the neck of a woman who bent
over a pad, sketching, but he showed neither weakness nor desire
and turned away almost at once, so indicating the ascetic limits of
earthly lusts. . . .

A peaceful English countryside witnessed the reappearance of
a Landru, under the name of Mahon. The same disappearances
of young girls, but the remains—more recent, incinerated or
buried by a more novice hand—are more eloquent.* The English
murderer is young, of cultivated intelligence, his face and speech
impress the audience : 'How pleasant he is! And such a gentle
appearance!' For tradition, and public naïveté, expect a murderer
to be branded with a bestial and violent face. A bestial and violent
man will go as far as to kill because he is under the influence of
drink, exasperated, or driven by rage and alcohol. He is paltry.
He does not know the pleasure of killing, the charity of bestowing
death like a caress, of linking it with the play of the noble wild
beasts : every cat, every tiger, embraces its prey and licks it even
while it destroys it.

* Patrick Herbert Mahon was hanged for the murder of his mistress Emily
Kaye, then in her late thirties, in September 1924. Though a philanderer,
Mahon was not responsible—so far as is known—for the 'disappearance of
young girls' or for any other murders.

Landru did not gain the benefit of irresponsibility; no doubt we shall see that Patrick Mahon, too, is of sound mind, intelligent, good-humoured. The fact is that neither of them is an accident of degeneration; they are survivors, relics. Possessors of an animality lost elsewhere, they radiate a gentleness full of shadow, bathed in the grace still possessed by those peoples chance has preserved from European contacts. Do we not know that Patrick Mahon had a singular attraction for 'hinds and stags and other wild animals'? The detail is worthy of note. I believe that no deeply civilized being can charm animals. An animal readily displays its distrust, that is to say its independence, of those entirely given over to humanity. Mahon charms animals; that appears to be a romantic feature to be added to the history of his crimes, whereas in fact it is one further abyss, and because of this I despair of his ever being able to make himself understood by an English jury, or even by a French jury.

The wild bird recognizes and follows him, flying above his head. At sight of him the dog's hair bristles upright along its back, it reflects and submits; the cat rubs itself against his leg as against a tuft of valerian; his mare, should he essay another mount, snorts with flared nostrils and lashes out with jealousy. . . . Fired by a rabble of obeisant creatures, desined to cause feminine rivalry, the ingenuous Patrick Mahon doubtless trod a happy road. A gentle monster, content with the facile act of killing, but whom our time constrains to maladroit and boring butchery. . . .

Marcel Schwob, who knew everything and guessed the rest, refused one day in the Tuileries to admire an old man, covered, like a dry tree, with tame birds. 'I don't like these bird-charmers,' said Marcel Schwob to his wife, Marguerite Moreno.*

She protested and he became incensed, as he never missed an opportunity to be. He uttered paradoxes in short bursts: 'No, I don't like them. They make me frightened. They are sadists. Bloodthirsty sadists. Torturers; and usually they murder children of both sexes, flay them methodically, and put them into round

---

* Marcel Schwob (1867–1905), of Jewish origin, was a critic prominent in the Symbolist movement. Marguerite Moreno (1871–1948), the actress, was a close friend of Colette; one of her most famous creations was the title role in Giraudoux's *The Madwoman of Chaillot*.

hat-boxes, which inevitably leads to the uncovering of their crimes, since during the transport of their victims, cut up into pieces, the string that ties the parcel slips and the whole lot is spilled into the street. . . .'

Animals

The fox-terrier of la Courtine has just miraculously escaped a double peril : the explosion of ten tons of dynamite and the unbridled curiosity of man. Stolen, it is restored to its master; thus its little romance is over, it ceases to be a matter for discussion. The other dogs, those that la Fourrière hands over to the laboratories, go on. Researchers, with science as their authority, will be able to cut them up, alive, into small pieces, drop them from a height to see if they are shattered by the fall, or deprive them of sleep for sixteen days and nights continuously for the purposes of an iniquitous monograph. . . .

Animal trust, undeserved faith, when at last will you turn away from us? Shall we never tire of deceiving, betraying, tormenting animals before they cease to trust us?

Our manner of exploiting domestic animals offends common decency. There is no forgiveness, according to peasant wisdom, for the proprietor who plays havoc with his own property. Yet one dare not say how many rustics, when their cow struggles to give birth and pants as it lies on its litter, take a cudgel, close the stable doors, and beat the cow so savagely and so fiercely that it finds the strength to get up, to try to flee, so that its despairing leap delivers it abruptly of its fruit, often inflicting mortal injury.

There will always be kids that arrive at the market hung up by their trussed tender feet, heads down, blinded with apoplexy. There will always be horses who, condemned to death, arrive at the place of their deliverance over miles of road, on three feet, on

bleeding unshod feet, their wretched flanks straddled by unfeeling
riders. The rabbit will always surrender its life with a frightful
scream, at the moment when the pointed knife puts out its eye and
penetrates its brain. The sensibility of our civilized tourists is out-
raged, in Africa, to see the sharp goad of the donkey-driver sink
into the donkey's open wound, carefully kept open; but just read,
in an illustrated magazine this month, about the method of catching, housing, feeding and finally disposing of ortolans! At first
they quiver in barred traps in their thousands when hardly bigger
than large hornets, then a dark loft awaits them where those cap-
tives who do not die consume a measured amount of food. There,
their health declines in a singular fashion that turns them into balls
of fat and their feathers sometimes fall spontaneously from their
stretched skin, as delicate as the membranes of bats. This is the
time—as the magazine conscientiously explains—to kill them by
'crushing their beaks'. A photograph shows us a good ortolan
killer, a model worker, who can crush the beaks of two birds at
a time. The work, paid at piece rates, breeds virtuosos; this one
smiles the smile of a fine fellow.

At the rate of two or three dustcarts a day the mounds of stones
removed from the fortified walls of Paris diminish before my
windows. They have been getting smaller for two years now and
I calculate that the operation may last another three at least. Each
morning the cart—the typical cart, the unique specimen, the cart
in fact—arrives empty. Two men fill it. The work of four human
arms, the operation does not proceed without slowness and rest
periods; I'd like to see you juggling with those ten-kilo blocks!
But the workers have perseverance, if not alacrity, and the cart
fills. Then one of the two navvies shouts 'Gee-up!' at the shaft-
horse, who's generally preceded by a lead-horse. The shaft-horse
leans all its weight on its collar, the lead-horse gathers itself on its
hind-legs, and . . . the cart doesn't move. For the earth of the
fortifications, a yellow clay softened by the slightest moisture, has
yielded during the loading to the deep imprint of the four wheels
and engulfs the cart a little more every minute. 'Gee-up!' Each
effort leads to another. The leather-thonged whips—I thought
they were officially forbidden—go to work. The yellow clay is like
a leech under the cart, sucking at the hooves, and the scene, pro-

tected from being overlooked by a high fence, assumes its traditional character of noisy torture. Helpless, glossy with sweat, with
bleeding stripes, these fine and desperate draught-horses endure
everything the human creature, ignorant of animals, ignorant of
the craft he claims to follow, can invent. On Thursday, if I
recollect aright, the departure of the filled cart took two hours
and the exhaustion of two prize horses. Two cubic metres of stone
went off at walking pace towards an unknown destination; their
driver, at any rate, tired by his exertions with voice and whip, did
not fail to stop at the first place for a drink.

It is an ugly sight to see an armed man treating a defenceless
animal severely. The inaction of the passer-by, detained by the
curiosity of an overloaded cart, constitutes one of the immoralities
of the street. Man has the right to rest before a working animal
only if the normal exertion of his servant produces normal results.
In my lilac-covered district I no longer care for the markets that,
twice a week, cause a bustle in our little provincial squares, their
walls overflowing with laburnum and paulownia. For the green
vegetables, ruddy carrots and pinkish potatoes, crimson-footed
rhubarb, the dressed meats, all the edible riches, all the expensive
victuals, arrive, I know, at the slow pace of teams sick of life and
bound for the slaughter-house. Whence comes this cruel indifference of the boss, the prosperous tradesman, the market-gardener
profiting from his garden or the buyer at les Halles, for his four-
footed employees? They are only rough donkeys, never groomed,
ill-fed horses. Canvas screens conceal—but I lift them—the col-
lapse of these screws while they munch at a pittance where an
oat-kernel is like a currant in a pudding and rest with one leg
across the other. Sometimes a dog drowses under the arch of their
belly. Horse and dog expect nothing of their master but his return.
But they would tell you that that's quite enough. They see him
return, full of shouts, mysterious, animated by inexplicable
caprice. They hear the sound he utters, ready to submit but not
to flee, they see in his eye the mood of the moment. Only a man
who has been chastised is capable of shunning man and hating
him.

It is man who has affixed the word 'wild' to the name animal.
About this, ask the opinion of those who have lived in solitude,

who have invaded a hitherto inviolate animal territory. Question the trapper spared and followed by the bear, the hunter surprised by the clemency of the wild beast and its condescending play. Without doubt they will teach you that we are the eternal curiosity, the unlucky passion of every animal, their treacherous climate, swollen with storms. Once they experience our daily inclemency they retain a nostalgia for it for ever. Subject to man's incomprehensible anger, if one should groan without trace of rancour 'Ah, what bad weather!', another will sigh with the despairing gratitude of an ill-treated lover, 'Still, it's better than nothing at all. . . .'

What did it want, the ocelot of the tropical forest, the wild creature splashed with black like a flower, when it purred all night beneath the hammock of the white hunter? It fled at dawn, for it possessed the timid feline heart oppressed by broad daylight and shy of revealing itself. Like every wild animal it had trembled at its first glimpse of man the unknown. It had guessed at impossible happiness and had manifested this in a medley of loud, raucous cries, insults and groans; it had scratched, licked, bitten and rubbed its head against the knees of The-one-who-never-understands. So it went away at dawn, having offered its trusting sleep, the soft murmur of its drowsy happiness, and the witness, imprinted in the grass, of its beautiful form, flanks long like the flanks of women.

Flowers

I dedicate to them, these imprisoned flowers, a little of the pity that goes out to caged animals. Almost alive as they are, these die the more quickly for having travelled, having found a miserly, shifting, shallow soil. As the plant perishes one can guess at the life it had there and how tenaciously it held on to it. Its flagging, the pathetic inclination of its floral head, constitute a genuine syncope, accompanied by pallor, since the plant now reveals the whiter underside of petals and foliage. If it receives watery aid in time, it is restored in the most dramatic fashion. How many moments have I lost—if I can call them lost—with flowers as avid for moisture as the anemone, the tulip, the hyacinth, the wild orchid! Swooning with heat and thirst, their stalks, plunged into water, imbibe so much, so greedily, that the energetic movement of the flower, its return to the vertical, become visible, jerky at first and by fits and starts when the head is too rich and too heavy.

It is a pleasure sweet to a writer to witness the rebirth of a tulip in a crystal goblet. The ink dries on the pen while before me a creation, interrupted by a transient death, raises itself towards perfection and will attain it, shine for a day, perish the next. . . . I can do better than watch the tulip regain its senses; I can hear the iris blossom. Its last protective silken layer rasps and splits down the length of an azure finger which uncoils at the proper time and, sitting by oneself in a small quiet room, one may start suddenly if one has forgotten that, on a nearby table, an iris has suddenly decided to blossom. Consider how there are, at the Cours-la-Reine, thousands of irises, renewed by continued flowering. The early morning sun delivers those whose time is come and I am seized with desire for that morning when, in the dawn that filters through the curtains, I may be able to cock an ear for the perceptible sighing of so many irises delivered simultaneously. . . .

They flower without pause, suffering too, so it seems, panting with their canine tongues hanging out—see the median vein, the ramifying canals, the fleshy and transparent border. It's their own perfume that suffocates them, so cloying is it; lingering, inclined to trail, closely seconded by that of the petunia. The bed of irises is a torpid pool that our passage cleaves with difficulty. Nervous women blanch there, pushing away with their hand the insupportably languorous perfume exhaled by all those heraldic tongues, some of which bear hairs like those of leopards. As for the roses, the female visitors extend not only their nostrils but also their mouths, as if at a fountain. After which these thirsty doves loudly proclaim the unprecedented odour of a new rose, the more beautiful for having gradually conformed to the will of a horticulturist who wanted it to resemble a peony, a hollyhock, the flat clematis or the double cherry.

One has the scent of well-cared-for skin, another of a mild cigar, or apricot or pineapple. But which of these equals a rose with the scent of a rose? Lips linger on the latter, nostrils flutter; the woman who inhales it closes her eyes: 'Leave me, I feel as if I had at last come home.' A home that she would endow with the names of Sensibility and Reverie and Literary Affectation, if she could but name it. But she knows only that the scent of the rose is enough to impregnate a woman with a vague and sibylline poetry, as if it were ten centuries ago.

For years now we've had no cause to mistrust the begonia. It has appeared as an emblem in the end-of-year reviews, where the lobster—hairy variety—has been of comparatively little account beside it. To suit popular caprice the begonia has developed strangely. Already, enlarged and cultivated, it resembled an exceptional begonia, then a monstrous begonia. This year we stand stunned before its megalomanic flower, which aspires to replace the hollyhock, the nasturtium, the peony, even the rose. A blaze of incomparable, presumptuous colours adorns it, it claims the most beautiful vibrant reds, a yellow that sheds light all round, a unique fleshy saffron. But smell it; it has less fragrance than a clod of earth and, if you touch it cautiously, it has been unable to lose its vegetable stiffness, its flesh as brittle as that of a young radish.

I have no time for these disguised vegetable characters. Those that puff themselves up so exaggeratedly leave me cold. Some growers miniaturize the brabancon and the fox-terrier, others bring a blush to the hydrangea. Let us be fair to the latter: they admit, even at their exhibitions, that they are not concerned with art. Here is the blue hydrangea alongside the pink, the purple-blue, then the white, arranged in kitchen-garden geometry; it's enough for each swollen head, with its globe of a flower erect on the stocky stem, to fill its compartment. Someone will be vexed— the chrysanthemum.

Something of romanticism embalms a rockery devoted to the spears, the bells of foxgloves. They remember their original sand, their fine burning natal soil, hot to the walker's foot in July. Their race has known the sun that calcines the rocks of Fontainebleau and they remain unbending beneath the stifling tent at noon. But dying and prostrate at their feet are the small scented folk, dull, delicate, ancient, provincial. They have names that stir the heart: herb-bonnet, sage, cinquefoil, lupin, the hairy cornflower. Yet who stops for these? A single gaping gloxinia could swallow them at a gulp. Beware the gloxinia! Velvety fat *arriviste*, it glares at the begonia. . . . Oh, to be the first to possess a gloxinia as big as a bedroom pitcher, what a dream!

At noon the little lotus-pool steams and there rises from the depths of the calyces the stagnant, somniferous odour that annihilates energy and appetite. Every flower cries for mercy, and the garden-lovers go to lunch. In the torrid, steamy enclave where the orchids are massed, 'the most beautiful flower' poses for its portrait. This prize beauty, a cattleya, proffers its certificates and swoons against a background of black velvet. Its foot is swathed in a silken binding, as it might be a prize charger. Around it there are only blue throats darting an inflamed stylus, wings barely retained on a threadlike stalk, ophrys and orchis camouflaged as striped fish, fruits, wine-coloured bees, humming-birds: vegetable contrivances, traps to catch butterfly, bird, insect, even man? What complicated design modelled the most cunning orchid of all, the most impenetrable, the one that succeeds in imitating—I give you a hundred guesses—the flat and honest corolla, the everyday mauve and commonplace blue of the simple pansy that flourishes in the nuns' small garden? . . .

Doubles

I should like to know what nostalgia is being experienced by the former cashier of the Opéra-Comique, now incarcerated.

Does he regret his honest life or the enchanted hours that saw him, suddenly long-haired, by the side of a young woman? Does he, so used to balancing accounts, say: 'It's worth having got rid of all that'? No doubt he mourns the chill conjugal dwelling and the esteem of the *quartier*. For the perverse regret their valley blessed with pure dew all the more, since the just do not aspire to such forbidden delights. M. Picard is perverse, there's no doubt of it. He was brought up in that school of demoralization constituted by an impeccable life, made up of amiable duties, beside a spouse beyond reproach. Before sinning officially he was acquainted with excess and intoxication, thanks to the inexorable repetition of the same daily virtues. Even wheels like a change of speed and, alas, nothing altered Picard's pace. We may wager that he took scant heed of the household set-up, that safety-valve for cramped bureaucracy. Sad rotation of the days, the slow vortex of wretched drunkenness, the sickening lack of colour in life, these are what corrupted Picard rather than the proximity of the theatre and the nearby costumier's. . . .

A young sage who died gloriously during the war, called Maitrot, taught boxing and physical culture. He judged all things soundly, from the height of shoulders fit to destroy a temple. He showed me great friendship, which I reciprocated, and it was he who dissuaded me from applying myself to sessions of slow, re-peated, rhythmic movements which I had essayed to overcome a keenly felt sorrow.

'None of that,' said Maitrot. 'Movements by numbers, they do those in school, in groups, in the open air and then it's when you've no worries. You're in trouble : no gymnastics with movements by numbers.'

'Why, Maitrot?'

'Because of the poisons. You see people who do what they call physical culture in movements by numbers. I count and count : one, two, three. . . . The stomach flattens, I admit, the poise improves, but at the same time the morale of these persons suffers, and their physiognomy too. "I don't know what's the matter with me," they say. They're suffering from self-induced neurasthenia. It's the poison that's in the numbers. Because, if you count you must do exactly the same movements over and over again, you poison yourself.'

'But how do you explain that, Maitrot?'

'I can't explain it. I'm sure, that's all. You want to beware of figures that you count out loud or softly, and of regular movements. The body isn't constructed for the same movements always, nor is the soul.'

Strange language from the mouth of an athlete, who thereby revealed a vocation as psychologist.

I have read, I don't know where, of an exemplary woman employee who suddenly threw down her work in the factory, insulted her bosses, and was seized with an acute nervous crisis because she had just calculated that she had finished her eight thousandth buttonhole. . . . Was it at the foot of a column of figures or else when greeting his concierge for the four thousandth time that Picard experienced his premonitory heart-sinking and revolt? He does not say so, he would not know how to say it. He talks instead of sentimental encounters, of falling head over heels in love, of frenzy. He would lack the words to explain how, suddenly, and to save his life, he had to jump into the skin and soul of another man. . . . But what other man? He had no choice. A bandit, his time up, allows himself the luxury of a sudden confession, drowned in blissful tears. Picard-cashier could not don a thief's disguise or Picard-husband become inconstant. He learnt what it costs to keep a secret and was eventually sufficiently shocked to admit everything. He managed, perhaps with a last touch of guile, to sacrifice the make-up box at the feet of his legitimate wife and, without the knowledge of his judges, to do penance to his directors, already disposed to clemency—he wants the public confessional, which he prefers to the simmering *pot-au-feu*, to the faithful lamp and companion.

Poor companion, sadly resembling the woman maligned by Marseille folklore in several bantering anecdotes:

'Hallo there, Marius.'

'Hallo there, Pascalin.'

'Is Madame Marius well?'

'Well, Pascalin.'

'Does she manage the house? Does she look after the cooking? Does she do her dressmaking?'

'Yes, Pascalin.'

'She looks after the children? In fact, she still has all the virtues?'

'Yes, Pascalin.'

'Hmm. . . . That's bad!'

It was not only with make-up, with false hair, with rouge to touch up a sagging mouth, that Picard manufactured his clandestine appearance, divulged by the newspapers. Colour and greasepaint would not have sufficed. But after applying the last touch of make-up he gave spontaneous life to the newly painted mask. The eye played tricks that he later forgot, the mouth, braced in its smile, resembled the underside of the chin, dragged the neck and shoulders into an attitude of defensive coquetry, his gait reacted to the carriage of his head, the bracing of the shoulders; then Picard left his hotel room, destined for another existence. Intoxicating departure, perhaps the best moment of the metamorphosis! For after this departure there came disquiet, fatigue, the summons to become a lover. . . . Only the moment of return could stand comparison with the dash of departure : the right, the pleasure to become old again, ugly again, to reclaim the bowl and the *tisane*, the security of having finished with deception until the morrow, all these relegated to second place the pleasures of imposture. To the gentle tinkling of the spoon against the cup of infusion, Picard enjoyed what was probably the cruellest moment of his destiny.

The assassination of a woman in a furnished apartment twenty years ago revealed the honourable name and the age of the victim, an octogenarian seductress, and her double life. More romantically than Picard, she died rather than called for the help that would have unmasked her. Some time later I was astounded to learn that I had met this heroine two or three times at the little family 'five o'clocks' at a friend's, where Madame . . . let's say Madame Protée, in triangular mourning shawl, *chapeau fermé* tied with a string over her white locks, rejoiced us with her gay grandmotherly vitality. She walked well and laughter dwelt in her wrinkles. A gourmande, she slowly savoured the creamy chocolate, eyes closed. Her duplicit maturity, based on firm decision, went on in strict parallelism interrupted only by her indiscreet death. A headstrong Ninon of Montmartre, she benefited also from the unassailable standing of a fairy grandmother and never got into any difficulties. She lived unsuspected on one or other side of the watertight division created, in their meticulous fashion, by her old hands. I have to take a good look at her, at the back of my memory, to remind myself how, eyes closed, a cup of chocolate between her gloved fingers, she sometimes seemed to abandon herself mysteriously to the two greatest sins of an elderly lady— *gourmandise* and reminiscence.

Cinema

No cars were parked at the entrance to the Musée Galliéra last Thursday; which led us to believe that the room reserved for 'Art in the French Cinema' would be empty. Just the reverse, it over-flowed beyond the doors with a silent audience of mingled children and adolescents. This fine and modest audience, which had arrived uncomplainingly under a hail of rain by slow and incon-venient modes of transport, close-packed now on the benches of a stifling room, received its just reward. Together we watched what is denied us by those screens where the only rivals to Ameri-can epics are *Didi découche* or *Patochard cherche sa belle-mère*. Two magic words had drawn me thither for I know that, cine-matographically, fantasy, marvels, incontestable miracles, are to be sought only in what is called the educational film.

One part of the presentation took us on tour in France, over the summits of low hills, along rivers sluggish in their flat, cramped valleys; as well as this, the tired voice of a teacher explained that the shape of these hills, this watercourse, these trees, depended on an invisible subsoil—cretaceous, siliceous clay. A field in the Perche showed proud draught-horses,* the satin of their coats gleaming and dappled over the play of muscle. In a granite quarry, stone-hewers lifted the blocks, carved out millstones with the chisel. . . . Schoolchildren ! Surely you will never forget the happy light, like that enveloping a soap-bubble, that shone on the cruppers of the horses with the aquiline foreheads, or the strange,

* *Percherons.*

many-toothed shape of a black tool biting into white stone; surely your memory will retain the movement of the quarryman's two dark gigantic hands which, before your very eyes, hacked the friable block, striped with pure white, to show you that kaolin is hidden away like truffles; that, like the truffle, it is invested with thick clay ! Children, from the height of a transporter-bridge you saw the wheat flowing like lava at the port of Marseille, in a wave so solid that we seemed to hear its aqueous murmur. . . . Children, resist those who still protest, in the name of the imagination, against teaching with the motion picture ! They are not fools or simpletons who assert : 'To feed the childish imagination with precise images is to deaden and restrict it. Teaching by cinematography turns the child into a receptacle for images and condemns every sense, save the visual, to inertia.'

At first sight this argument does not seem negligible. For our civilized senses lose no chance of impoverishment. I am assured that, deprived of music, cinema-halls would become the agents of communal slumber; I am also assured that, confronted with a film, the child hardly thinks at all. It may well be that it thinks very little, faced with some confused activity where human movement has pride of place. The beating of the heart, the to-and-fro of the eyes, supplant thought while the screen is showing the hero pursued by kidnappers or murderers and revolver shots explode in wads of cotton-wool. The interruption of the subtitles suffocates like a stoppage of breath and I'm inclined to believe that the child's mind finds no place to settle therein or to turn fruitfully inward. The exciting film, rapid pursuits, all those sports whose speed surpasses the normal rhythm of our heart and lungs, eliminate those thoughts that are not mere recording or painful pleasure.

But give the child, the adult too, cinema spectacles devoid of romantic action; neither the child nor the adult will be niggardly in expressing his surprise, the quality and vividness of his pleasure and interest. I recall, during the showing of the film called *Way Down East*, that the audiences, each evening, gave voice like one man to a long murmur of appreciation at an incomparable countryside, silvered by the rising sun, of quivering willows and a great river, soaked by the morning dew. Despite the courage and talent of Lilian Gish, it was here that the emotion of the moment found its sigh, its release and regrets.

Similarly, last Thursday at the Musée Galliéra, there were two moments when every young hand clapped, when mouths exhaled their content, their 'Ah' of respectful ecstasy. The first time, in slow-motion, a sea-gull was lifted from the ground, immobilized in the air, cradled in the wind. The undulation and banking of its wing-quills, the mechanism of its tail rudder, the whole secret of flight, the whole simple mystery of aviation, were revealed in an instant, dazzling the eyes. A little later the speeding-up process recorded the germination of a bean, the birth of its searching rootlets, the greedy yawning of its cotyledons from which, darting its snake head, the first shoot burst forth. . . . At this revelation of the plant's purposive, intelligent movement I saw children get up and imitate the prodigious ascent of a plant climbing in a spiral, circumventing an obstacle, groping at its stake. 'It's looking, it's looking!' cried an impassioned small boy. He dreamed of it that night, and I too. These fantasies are not forgotten and excite a hunger to learn more. We desire for our children and ourselves, we desire, after the poor workings of one's imagination, the extravagance of reality, Nature's unrestrained fantasy; we desire the fantastic fable of the germination of the pea, the marvellous story of the metamorphosis of a dragonfly and the explosion, the forceful expansion of the lily-bud, half-open at first with its long mandibles on a sombre swarm of stamens, an avid potent process of flowering, at sight of which a little girl said quietly, rather scared : 'Oh, a crocodile!'

Spells

The brother of a soldier, killed in the war, has the use of the dead man's bicycle. He has a fatal fall, leaving the bicycle to a newspaper-seller who is knocked down and run over by a lorry. The fourth owner of the bicycle, chased by the police for burglary, runs away; he is arrested, but the policeman who rides the 'fatal bicycle' to the police-station is knocked down and run over by a car. . . .

This is a jolly story that comes to us from England, country of the haunted castle and the malevolent opal. Over there the vampire is still in good standing. But if there were a possibility of buying the bicycle in question, would you buy it? Not I. And I would not wear the malevolent opal on my finger, if I knew the history of the bicycle and the ring. I can't help thinking that the last victim, the policeman, had the time before straddling his mount to become acquainted with its fatal power. He was responsible for his own downfall; I believe that, instead of giving way to the car, instead of crying '*Hep!*' in English (I don't know how one says '*Hep!*' in English), he had a moment of indecision, despite himself, and the car was on him. . . . Note that on each occasion the bicycle remains more or less intact; I stress this point so as to evoke in my readers the realm of the fantastic and the damnable pleasure savoured by the superstitious. The gleam of planetary fire that ravages the opal, that I am not afraid of. I mistrust only the opal of evil repute, the ring that your grandmother wore on her finger when she lost her life on a boat-trip and that she herself had had from a mysteriously murdered grandmother. But the bracelet of woven hair inspires no more confidence in me than the opal, once I know that these threads of tarnished gold were cut under the Restoration from the tresses of a dying fiancée, a fiancée who, a fiancée whom. . . .

Haunted houses, now those I know something about. The rat behind the panelling runs in a hundred surprising ways, and when he plays, his shrill little rat's laugh makes the hair of the unsuspecting stand on end. The death-watch beetle, terrifying name, is to its familiars only an insect set on banging its head against the wall, a head shaped like a hammer, hard as the wood it taps at regular intervals: toc-toc-toc-toc-toc-toc-toc, often in a series of seven. Ah! You prick up your ear! Seven? Why seven? I couldn't say. The tropical gecko also cries seven times and when it goes beyond this number someone dies in the house. . . . You shiver, eh? Under pretence of reassuring you I fill you with new terrors.

Let us speak of other charming hosts who, come summer, assume the responsibility of maintaining the reputation of their castles, English or otherwise, the great grasshopper with a horse's head and the stag-beetle whose horn scrapes against the window-pane in the dark or on the wood of the table like a scratching finger-nail. Let us mention the gently sobbing owl, capable, when flying against your face in the darkness without so much as a sigh, of imitating the fold of a shroud or the icy breath of the tomb! Four or five small twilight or nocturnal animals, an artfully modulated draught, and that's goodbye to the case of the haunted house, at least the haunted houses one talks about and which receive noisy publicity. There are others. . . . There are dwellings saturated in defunct humanity, the murmuring overflow of unknown souls. Sometimes beneficent, sometimes lethal, these dens crammed with an invisible population make their influence felt on the insensitive living—you, I, our neighbour, our friends— who translate it into inadequate words: 'I don't know what's the matter with me, I feel uneasy in my new room . . .'; or else: 'I feel much better in my new house. I'm not so irritable any more.'

One of these places, favoured by one who shall be nameless, is well known to me. A dark courtyard obscures the view and the friend who moved in there parcelled out in a single day all the furniture, the divan-bed, desk and ash-trays. It took us only forty-eight hours to discover that a guardian spirit had settled in before the furniture: a spiritual warmth, unobtrusive company, encouragement that came from no one knew where, an even respiration of the walls accustomed to human contact, nothing was lacking in this basement dwelling, scorned though it was by the sun. Then who was haunting it? A single former inhabitant, even one of the powerful dead, would not account for it. I may happen to sleep there for half an hour, a sleep well watched over, or to eat there with a motiveless cheerfulness, while the detestable mezzanine light, obliquely filtering in, stagnates in grey splashes at the bottom of the white plates. . . . Quite different is the almost rural comfort of my little house in Auteuil, blessed by thrushes and nightingales. No doubt, both here and there, a closed door there, a bed of climbing roses here, is found the one whom I designate in all seriousness by his name—the vampire.

Ah! Now we have it! Honour to whom honour is due, the greatest and the most frightening. You can tell him thus. Pale, a little green even, hands . . . and with a mouth like a wound, right? Your guess is too crude, all the same. It's very likely that your most ostentatious vampire is no more than a harmless candidate for tuberculosis, enhanced by Peladan's great eyes and a hair-do that I used to say was a chemist's before chemists became sporting types. Your true vampire, unhappily for his victims, dispenses with outward characteristics. He usually has a fresh complexion, a smiling approach, a wandering eye. If it is a woman she is charming, idle, gay, with an infantile manner of devoting her time, her presence, to admiring and liking you. The male vampire presents the same absence of special features and the same amiable manner. Man or woman, the vampire is generally liked. His most frequent phrase is 'What shall we do?' For he awaits some motivation, he seeks it if necessary. Like every incarnation of shabby fiendishness, he is 'nice'. Very nice, and you say so, you repeat it *ad nauseam*. You seek the vampire, who is seeking you. Whenever he departs he leaves you depressed, yawning by fits and starts, saddened as if by a debauch. He takes away everything you need, everything that assures his subsistence, and it may be that as he leaves he will get further plunder on his way, using the residue of your own energy. Will you die? No. Besides, an access of energy may save you, realizing that the vampire, uncertain how long to stay, will not desert your dried-up veins of his own accord. But you will measure your effort by the calibre of your enemy, his leechlike prowess, the frightful trap of his vacuity which you fill, blindly, with the best part of yourself.

Pedagogy

June : month of cherries and strawberries and the first bats ! All the nests are empty, the rose condescends to all our suburban gardens, prisoned between four walls. Bagatelle is ablaze with roses, a profusion of roses loads four wooden arches behind my house. Unbending roses, upright on their inordinate stems, at the large florists and short-stemmed roses on the hawker's tray, cheaper than leeks, which are also trussed in bundles. Hot roses, crucified against villa walls, exhausted by the sun. Plump, flushed roses, pride of the level-crossing keeper : 'They haven't any at the château like these'; the poor man's wild roses smelling of spring-onion because of the hand that picked them, the rich man's roses, one of the latest inventions, no bigger than a bee, simple, red, slender, whose yellow bristly heart, all hairy with stamens, releases such a wild fragrance as to be almost embarrassing. This is the month when the rose, blooming everywhere else, deserts our children's cheeks.

They reach, thank God, the third month of their longest term and can do no more. The majority do not suspect this. My sturdy daughter, who in any case has the advantage of a suburban school, betrays unknowingly and obviously the signs of what I call, each year, the inanition of these children. For them the school year is the boundary of their entire existence. October, mild for those children under the serene influence of a well-run boarding-school, brings the fluttering of wings, the trepidation, the excitement that flushes the baby at his first unaided steps. . . . Christmas fosters in them romanticism and lust for love; from that time on they grow up very quickly under thaw and shower; with good luck Easter lures them on with a St Martin's summer. May, June frankly display their fatigue, a sort of sensible or agitated disenchantment. This child of mine debates with her seasonal malady, triumphs over it, outpaces it; but it follows her, it catches up with her, and she lets herself be caught, though she does not officially admit its presence. She says : 'It's funny, I don't enjoy myself as much as

in winter and yet here we are starting a newspaper, Jacqueline
and I.' She says : 'You know, I haven't got the same best friend
any more. Why?—Oh, I don't know! And yet I thought she was
the best.'

She arrives tempestuously, crying : 'We've got two days' holiday! And do you know why? Because of Doumergue! That's a
good effort of his. Oh yes, now we want to make a revolution so
that they have a new President again, and we shall get another
two days' holiday!' But the access of joy is short-lived and the
signs of rejoicing subside in diminishing outbursts. The cinema,
the bicycle ride, I throw these at her like mouthfuls of water to a
fever case. I know that all this, to be truthful, is lustreless, done
with, hardly gayer than the daily grind. I know that one should
change the year, emigrate to a new world, emigrate to a new
world and die at this time.

Here and there people complain about exhaustion, demand
release. Hot weather régime, cold weather régime, no doubt that's
what studious youth demands, embedded in a teaching cycle that's
too old, that successive ministers approach with uncertain hands.
The retarding cold, the sleepy heat, the spring, languorous or
unsettling, we adults quite rightly put up with their effects and
blame them for our exhilaration or our listlessness. . . . Fatigued
by its own growth, our child, however, must contribute the same
amount of work throughout the year, the same in dog-days or
frost. The hard, the blind rule that sets a little girl of thirteen, a
boy of the same age, before an exercise-book at 30° C., at the
hour when the birds fall silent and the blue blind stops rattling
against the window-pane! What mature man, what oldster forgets
the particular temperature of his summer *baccalauréat* or dip-
loma? Yet, sheltered by an age not yet affected by dreams of
university, we witness the prodigies of resistance attained by our
offspring; we are compelled to admire them when we run through
the students' manuals and exercise-books: 'This is really too
much! A grown-up couldn't cope with it!' Let us admit that only
a child can cope with it. What memory, what resilience! It's time
we no longer abused a cerebral malleability that is not unlimited
and is endangered by prolonged and sterile effort.

Almost all the modern educational establishments deal with

the situation by using short and varied lessons. The sterile effort, so terribly demanding of the young spirit, results from causes not envisaged in educational circulars. Initially, the child is vulnerable only through his senses. Later his intelligence benefits from an enlarged sensibility. But at the beginning of his time at school some blemish or physical tic apparent in his teacher, some peculiarity of accent or pronunciation, may sometimes lose the teacher the interest and attention of his entire class. Ragging of the teacher by pupils, violent insubordination, spring from a secret horror—visual, olfactory, auditory—that the child will not acknowledge even to himself. Always unfortunate and less well rewarded than a rejected suitor, that is the mysteriously stricken pedagogue who imposes and engenders sterile effort. The pupil hears him without understanding. Trustingly the pupil raises to his master a petrified visage that supplicates and suffers before subsiding into an unhappy indifference. Hours, months, pass thus, the teacher vainly expending his magnetism, the pupil his attention. Their opposed forces are dissipated to little advantage. How many actors there are who can tell you that at certain times in their career they despatched to the other side of the proscenium words whose phonetic value and meaning were suddenly lost in the void?

This phenomenon of ingratitude is commoner, more constant, at school than in the theatre. As abettors of juvenile exhaustion and waste of time, oughtn't we to deal with it? I think so. Perhaps, if pedagogy sprang from vocation rather than ambition and if higher education produced graduates experienced in the art of addressing a crowd of children. . . . What then, a *Conservatoire* for teachers? Certainly. To talk to a child, to fascinate him, is much more difficult than to win an electoral victory. But it is also more rewarding.

Tits

The poplar seed no longer clouds the air, so light as to indicate the direction of the wind even when we do not feel the wind itself. It is the sweet of the year and sappy, ephemeral blossomings accompany it—hyacinth, narcissus, tulip. It is composed of discordant greenery, various as a lawn of silver-green or jonquil-green, of pimento-green to bluish-green : the Parisian Bois has just reached its fugitive maturity.

By now spring would be over for us had not the tits, because of the cold, been late with their hatching and the sparrows too. It's not ten days since the befeathered little tits jostled each other in their nests. And if my narrow garden retains till June the charm of an uncultivated tomb, abandoned of men, it will be because all work with spade and rake has been deferred, silenced, round a nest of tits.

What harshness is needed, I asked myself, to lose the trust of animals? Refinements of torture are vain and never exile an animal long from us. A kindly gesture bestowed by us on an animal arouses prodigies of understanding and gratitude. When I fixed two nests hollowed out of two birch billets to two uprights in the garden I secretly thought of them as a superstitious votive offering. . . . The vow knows only one path, it rises; mine reached two wall-nightingales. They came, greyish-red, darker than the shrew but, like it, a forager, and began their delicate pillage all about the house under my inspecting eye. One day the round window of the nest was blocked by a thread of floss-silk, stolen from a blouse. . . . This pink thread, as it floated there, spoke as clearly as the lace curtain in the window of an apartment : I behaved circumspectly, especially as the other nest belonged at the same time to a blue tit.

The latter, princess of wild birds, can do nothing without *éclat*. Where she reigns one sees only her, her back blue as the metallic wing-case of the dung-beetle, the willow-green underside of her wing, her brazen begging, her quickness to flee. She is laughing and combative and greedier than anyone. Would you say she is

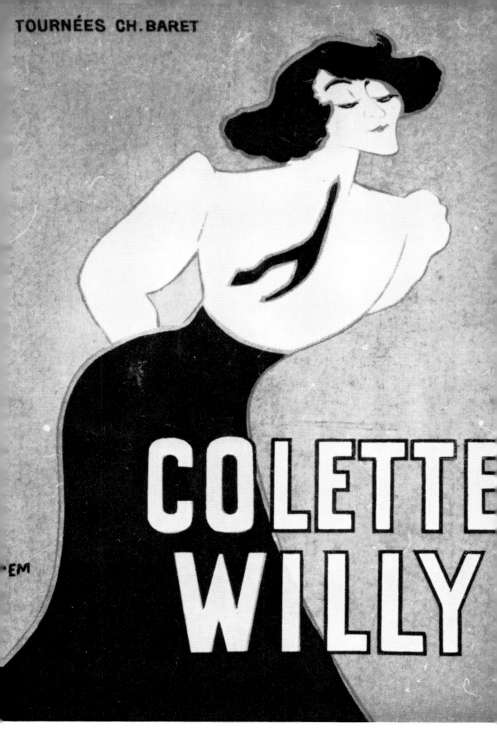

TOURNÉES CH.BARET

COLETTE WILLY

Poster for a music-hall tour by Colette, the work of the famous
caricaturist Sem

Colette in her orchard

fierce? But it is man who speaks thus and how can a man have any idea of what a tit's fierceness may be? It hunts and scavenges from waking to sleeping and it goes to sleep late. Between the hatching of its eggs and the flight of the fledglings its daily round defies observation. Two blue flashes, blurred by the swiftness of their flight, lit up for me my small burgeoning enclosure. Male and female, just as they disappeared into the round window of the hollow trunk, perched for an instant on the end of a bamboo stake and swayed there like a flower; their brood fed, the sound of a fan, a streak of blue and yellow fire shot out of the nest again and the waiting raised the pitch of the piping little invisible ones, which resembles the twitter of an exasperated kiss.

As for the more audacious and active, the small female, I've seen her dive beneath the low jungle of crowded young begonias. She entered at one end of the flower-bed and hunted about there like a rat, running agilely on her marvellous little claws; she shot out at the other end, arrogant, head erect, a caterpillar dangling from her beak or else moustached with two insect-wings, belli-cose. . . . Did she find the time to eat? No doubt, since she found time to sing again. Her little copper-coloured sistrum interrogated me, she feigned anger if I approached the nest. But it was only a tit's play, followed by acrobatics of amity and association—head down, hanging by her feet, swaying with a thousand flirtings of her tail and chucklings. Fierce? Perhaps. The tit is as gay as a wild beast. It is meticulous in the manner of those model housekeepers who fly into a rage if there is a stain on the parquet: the threshold of her nest does not bear a trace of white droppings. Fierce? How pretty she is when she kills! The worm snatched, she finishes it off with repeated blows and cuts it up with an executioner's fairness. Fierce, yes, no more and no less than innumerable lovers. . . .

For I've not been able to regard my tits' maternal instinct as a fault. The gardener sent for, they summed him up in five minutes, well aware that he smelled of earth and leaves and that he brought to light, shifting compost in a wheelbarrow, new plump vermin. The cat they had long ago forgotten, knowing their nest to be out of reach. They merely chose, to get the little ones to take their first flight, breakfast-time when the sun is low and the garden deserted and flew off to the wooden belfry.

J.F.M.—E

But I was rewarded more than once, until last week, at the edge of the racecourse. Nothing indicates to the eye a nest of tits abandoned by its brood, but the surrounding racket is news enough. . . . What cries! A constant high-pitched pedal-note of inharmonious squalling, fed by unmatchable vitality, emerges from the tree that bears the nest. Thin as a small cigar, grey still, a glimpse of yellow beneath the wing that beats as quickly as a butterfly's, the little birds quiver with emulation, turn by turn, on the edge of the natal chalice, felted with wool, floss-silk, selected moss and horsehair. The mother warbles on a twig, repeating a lesson that can readily be translated: 'No flying now! Or you'll catch your wing on the first branch and you'll be on the ground, in the grass, where I can't help you. One little jump only, with me. . . . Then another jump on the twig above, and another, another, always higher, to the top of the tree. . . .'

She bosses about four or five ignoramuses, scolds them, encourages them, shoves them with her wing, infects them with her own enthusiasm, leads them on, exhausted, to the top whence one can discern the green racecourse at Auteuil furrowed with birds.

There, momentarily, they are all silent. Is it vertigo that keeps them quiet? They contemplate the open air, the virgin territory that is theirs from now on. Is this not the moment of the greatest anxiety for the tit, blue amid her grey nestlings? Brief anguish. One of the little ones takes off from the tree, aims at an isolated chestnut-tree on the lawn, follows a course like a racing yacht, and berths triumphantly. Never, in three nests, have I come across any hesitation, any appeal for help, from the timorous young sparrow. The tits are expert in the air and gymnasts on the branches. Birch-trunk or hanging cradle, the natal nest never sees them again. They depart before their blue wing-quills have yet developed, pilferers, throaty, intoxicated with combat and coquetry, and capable of devouring, through its round eye-socket, the brain-substance of their own kind.

Heat

The torment of heat is reserved for the city dweller and the inhabitant of the desert, for more than elsewhere the mineral kingdom lends the sun's fury an implacable character.

For a few days in the desert I have experienced the mounting heat, received and reflected by a soil from which the scorching sun raised a spiral pillar of sand. But at least, at Bou-Saâda, the Saharan night shed its few hours of clemency, the cold that assumes a violet colour in the mind as it descends with night from the mountain-tops. Paris, during the dog-days, knows no truce, no relief for its affliction. We are a poor lot, who go about in winter wearing silk stockings and pierced leather shoes, and in summer in sleeved jackets, collared, tied and waistcoated. A poor lot? Why pity them? They have the elegance and the correct clothing that they deserve and have themselves chosen. The heat in Paris is like a nightmare. Thousands and thousands of human beings at their windows have nothing to look at but stone prisons, quadrangular blocks, rectangles of hot zinc, cubes of iron or cement. When the thermometer shows 'despair in the shade' there is something inexorable in all this cubic limit of gaze. I once knew an office where men suffocated from June on and where, when they looked up, they saw through some railings, a long dark corridor of a courtyard dominated by a tall white chimney, struck by the sun on its widest aspect during the latter half of the day. Deadly succession of right-angles! If, during these torrid months, plant-life is as necessary to us as nourishment, it is because it contains and engenders an inexhaustible supply of curves. 'Mercy!' begs dried-up man, 'a glass of fresh water—cylinder or circumference to ease the soul. . . .' I don't forget to rest my eyes and my brain on spheres of crystal and glass, the year round.

In our city, alas, each guild gets cooked in its own way : the one in trousers of thick stiff corduroy, the other in jackets with sleeves worn by the wood of desks. The caged book-keeper is half-dead in his detachable collar, and the saleswoman totters at her post in

the obligatory black dress with no comfort but the stoical gaze of
the frock-coated overseer, pale and choked, upright like the legen-
dary dead man, secretly pouring with sweat. In our country the
torrid noontide demands the same activity, the same toiling mass
is exposed, to perish under ever crueller rays, and each human box
harbours within its thin walls dazed sufferers, children to whom
night brings no repose, who utter their small, repeated cry till
dawn.

Cast a glance at the working-class houses, the tops of the thickly
populated buildings : no shutters, blinds that dim the light but
admit the heat. Those roasted on the fifth floor think with envious
ill-will that the ground-floor tenant leads a privileged existence in
a cellar. Soon we may see the last of those ancient Parisian buildings, entrenched camps of microbes but thick bastions where the
temperature fluctuates hardly more than that of the stone cham-
bers in the tower of Elven, in Brittany. In summer their deep
carriage entrances are the shady paradise of the seated concierge
and of a few elderly women with shade-spotted hands. A draught
from the tomb emanates from these entrance-ways in July and
brushes the forehead of the passer-by, who slackens his step, sighs,
and foresees for himself too, beyond the tomb, the eternal happiness of the man seated at a cool threshold.

On the evening of the terrible Saturday of 12th July even
Auteuil was no better off than the boulevards, and its inhabitants
complained angrily that the sun poured down on them the same
heat as on the natives of the 9th *arrondissement*.

Your born Auteuillois tends to the sybaritic, since he possesses
the Bois and its lakes. Basically a villager, he still speaks of 'going
to Paris', defends himself as best he can against sporting activities,
and pities the 'centre', not without malice. But he becomes indig-
nant when, as on the other day, the sultry weather does not, in
respect for the 'seventeenth', halt at the level of the way that an
aged kinswoman, ten years ago, used to call the 'Grande-Rue' of
Passy.

Accustomed, after dinner, to inhale the scent of limes, of privet,
of mown grass brought to its door by the faint west wind that has
caressed the Bois, Auteuil—deceived, injured—lived very meekly
indeed on that Saturday night. Around half past ten I went, at the

pace of the condemned, to see what was going on in Passy. The whole of Passy was lying prostrate on the burnt grass around la Muette, and the motionless body of some woman, lying face downward, her head between her crossed arms, seemed a victim of death rather than sleep. The lovers I saw all lay apart. No gaiety rose from the families who had eaten there, amid the greasy wrappings and the melon-rinds. Sometimes, in the half-shade, there sprang up some slender, light young girl, whose youth still impelled her to run and jump, but like the Olympic champions she suddenly sank down again, her white dress subsiding like the last flame of an unfed fire.

Round a shady green bush five or six silent beings resembled those who warm themselves at a winter brazier, intent on profiting from a singular cold radiation, a concentric zone of coolness of which the bush was the mysterious centre. A woman held out her bare arm, a child its two hands, and for a moment I shared their patch of oasis.

An arriving 16 tram took me back towards Auteuil. The imminence of midnight, and of Sunday, was reviving some village life despite the still air and dust-white sky. A little dance to lantern-light, not far from the avenue Mozart, resembled all the Saint-Jeans, all the fourteenths of July, of my natal province, and I was glad that the tram stopped just there. What honest youth! They danced among themselves, free from intrusion, the draper's daughter in the arms of the cooper's son, the jobbing dressmaker with her female apprentice, two little girls of ten did the polka, and the blonde servant-girl from the tobacconist's whirled round grasped by the smart waiter from the café.

Seltzer water, grenadine, beer, syrup of lemon. . . . The smell of the pine-branches nailed to the musicians' platform reminded me of beflagged fairgrounds, prizegivings and polished dance-floors. . . . Nothing was missing from this conjured past, not even the trusting parents sitting in a row on yellow iron seats.

From the height of the platform of the empty tram I breathed in this peaceful past and present. The young folk were dancing on the tramlines and I was not sorry that our halt was prolonged. At last I spoke to the conductor, leaning contemplatively, like me, on his elbows :

'Is there a breakdown along the line?'

'No. We'll be getting going again.'

'When?'

'In just a minute. We're waiting.'

'Waiting for what?'

'For them to finish their fox-trot. We didn't want to disturb them.'

Conflicts

'You're looking forward to getting there?'

'Oh yes, Mama!'

She dreams, and does not enlarge on her tepid acquiescence.

'Are you thinking about the sea, the beach, the terrace?'

'Oh yes, Mama!'

'What's the first thing you want to see?'

The hazel eye sparkles, a dimple hollows the right cheek, a childish glow reveals that this is the face of a little girl of eleven.

'I'm going straight away to see if the shell is still in the little blue box, and the sea-horse I painted green!'

She bounds up on both feet and goes away and the friend who is visiting me follows her with a condescending look: 'She's rather babyish for her age, isn't she?'

To which I reply with an offended mother's 'Yes, thank heavens!' Purely reflex on my part, as I'm not offended. It's a long while since I troubled to explain the child to grown-ups. I've been too occupied in understanding her myself. Left alone with my child I'd have refrained from asking so many inane questions, the equivalent of: 'Hold out your paw, nicely now!' I consider that my daughter did well enough, from respect and politeness, to speak in suitable terms while keeping to the truth.

Yes, sure enough, she'll go first to find her blue box, with its sleeping shell. Unique, heavily symbolic, the ritual objects dwell in a secret cupboard. When my daughter arrives at the weathered shore of the Ile-et-Vilaine she won't run to the romantic headland to claim from the sea the sea of yesteryear. She is too removed from our simplicity, which has no more need of symbols. Each season brings her nearer to it; high school, with its civilizing influence, makes her ever more ordinary. Nowadays she utters opinions which are the opinions of a clique, a sect, a group; she may even share them, that's her right. We have just extracted a few neutral words from her, but she is well aware that her silence is her own. It is there that she gambols in security, there that she ripens in awareness of risk and responsibility. We respect, she and I, the boundary I guard so jealously of the two mental domains, hers and mine.

Children! . . . Where you are concerned we can only wander undecidedly, advance gropingly. How does it happen that, in bringing you into the world, we lose that shrewdness of recollection that would enable us to understand you? We lose it for ever, a total obliteration; we lose it like the knack of flight that comes to us in dreams, as the new-born loses its knack of swimming a few hours after birth. Chance, rather than perspicacity, allows us to rejoin, to understand children; then they are our ephemeral conquest. A gentle patience works with them, but not more than a strong hand. We are disgusted by the brutality of some parents, yet without reflecting that this verbal brutality and its accompanying harshness of feeling are neither more nor less unproductive than a more seductive strategy. The words brim with antagonism. . . . Alas, one must struggle with what one loves, in love as in motherhood. Yet love adapts itself in *grosso modo* fashion and for a long while possession may suffice as final settlement.

'Trust . . . an open heart, the delightful blossoming of the child in the maternal breast . . . the crystal-clear spirit of the child. . . .' Literature is quite dewy with such expressions. I sometimes wonder whether this kind of doting writer ever had children. At other times I begin to doubt their sincerity as much as their intelligence. A troubled faith usually binds the child to its parents. A faith that suffers and has need of heroes and saints as it contemplates human failings. We can never be great enough for our sons, even

if the best they recognize in us evokes a filial fanaticism within
them. But fanaticism is a matter of pride. Between doubt and
fanaticism there is barely room for tenderness; slow to well up in
childish hearts, born of grief, sometimes of deserved punishment,
almost never of joy, it is a consolation that ripens late. Arbitrary,
as independent of our merits and virtues as love itself, it manifests
itself as timidly as love and heralds the first crack in the inexorable
serenity that haloes childhood. It is the weight of tenderness that
draws hitherto intact young creatures towards the weakness of
confidences, which are to trust what the fitful light and shade of
a shutter flapping in the wind are to broad daylight. The dawn of
victory for us, a happiness we must keep hidden—however, the
struggle starts again, the stern thrilling struggle. I dramatize? No
doubt. The truces, the happy surprises, make me tremble more
than need be, certainly more than is apparent. What deep love
can dispense with an atmosphere of drama? The extravagant
desire to give all, poisons motherhood, as if to punish it for its
passionate origins. But from the earlier flame what remains to the
mother is that the child is more demanding than the lover, and
will not share; that it chooses among the gifts one thinks to offer
it; that it remains inflexible where a lover would forgive, for a
child hugs its grievance, fixes it in memory, disinters it twenty
years later, fresh, gorged with a mysterious, vampiric life. . . . So
the mother refines and purifies within herself what love has left
untutored, rudimentary. An incorrigible lust for giving will always
attach itself to her like a blemish. But little by little she gives up
demanding tear for tear, transport for transport. More patient,
she will accommodate the good that she would once have ravaged
in amorous fury. The repeated check shapes her, at last she
acknowledges the mystery of the loved creature, she who but
recently tested her beloved prey with sight and scent, she who
could see a square of paper in a pocket gleaming through the
material, she who used 'Why?' and 'What are you thinking
about?' and 'Do you love me?' like a double-edged weapon. She
is proud to sport an appearance of reason every time in her life
that she thinks of renouncing the possessive spirit. . . . As if she
were capable of anything other than possession! No matter. An
ageing adversary, faced with a child in whom, the better to wound

her, there flourishes all that got the better of her, she savours the profits and perplexities of her practised tactics. For her there is no longer any equal footing. For in that period when her living creation relaxes and surrenders, during the peaceful seasons when youth refreshes itself, when the child returns to childhood, the mother secretly appropriates what she likes best and delights in it. 'You exist. Every moment you demonstrate my capacity. The fact is that you can do nothing against me, except to make me suffer. So long as you exist, I am the stronger. You are the owner of that cheek, that updrawn lip, that eye shaded in its deep socket, and that fresh-complexioned expression : so many weapons that will be fatal to others, but thank God I've already succumbed to them, for years now, and it is almost to defy you that I find, in what was once my downfall, my present fortune and subsistence. . . .'

Summer

Another year for octopuses. They reduce the number of shrimps and little rock-fish of the coast. I try to learn from them something of their nature; but my patience is exhausted by their astonishing sagacity. Should I forage for a little while with a shrimping-net in the submerged 'wharf' of a lobster or conger-eel, a strange caress gropes at my ankle in the green water, a delicate, cautious en-twining that suddenly clasps round my leg a fetter at once soft and burning, like certain flat water plants, whose stickiness does not allay its smarting : it is the arm of a little octopus, that is only induced to untwine itself because its prey is too large for it.

If, at low tide, I hold the baited shrimping-net at the edge of a salt pool, the agate shrimps come to palpate the raw meat with the tips of their bristles. They dance their shrimps' dance, one leap forward, two leaps back. In the middle of their transparent body a bright jade-green phial marks their full stomach. Intelligent, they pose themselves with bravado on my bare foot dabbling in the pool and stab it with their inoffensive beak. A sea-perch, all head and fanned-out fins, whisks its short tail, demands to be caught, if only for a moment; but who's interested in this inedible hog-fish? Even the cats won't have it. Dreamily, floating askew, heavy and agile, the 'clenched fist' then reveals itself and grasps the bait with an assured pincer. But it surveys us from below upwards, its articulated crab's eyes study our movements, it listens to us thinking and at its own pace regains the shadow to change into a pebble, a weed, an eddy of sand. It made no attempt to slice, with one scissor-stroke, the shrimps prancing on their own, or the little sea-perch, and I've never managed to surprise the struggle between the species which do, however, feed on one another. . . .

Betrayed by the crab, I often remain empty-handed beside my empty net and the mocking quadrille of shrimps. The weather is mild, the wind brushes the grubbing of potatoes, the upturned earth, the hay and the damp seaweed. . . . It's always just when my thoughts desert my half-hearted fishing that a firm grasp seizes the edge of the net and tests it with a brief shake. A long blackish finger, two, three long blackish fingers, of an indescribable heart-stopping suppleness, are knotted round the iron crown of the net; another reptilian finger, directed over the pocket, prods the meat bait, tugs at it, calls yet another finger to its aid. Should the meat yield to this tearing, the slender, studded, powerful fingers carry it off in one go. Should it resist, they are guided by a kind of fury. One attacks the meshes, tears, and carries off with the scrap of raw beef the bottom of the net. But neither during its approach nor in the course of the struggle have I seen the centre of the octopus, the thinking nucleus of the eight arms, the creature's cold and placid eye. It despatches the active parts of itself to a distance, recalls them, magically projects them. Small as it is, it sometimes excites in us a giddiness that is entirely cerebral, for its suckers are not tenacious and they are inoffensively pneumatic. It succeeds by fascinating the sea creatures, overcoming enemies of superior strength. I watch in vain for an encounter with an accustomed antagonist, I wait for its tentacles to seize its marine prey before my eyes. When we make an appearance it seems that all struggle ceases between wild animals, aquatic or terrestrial, that they shiver with a shared anxiety at sight of their common enemy, man.

On the other hand, our presence stirs up the quarrels of domestic animal with domestic animal. For a fortnight there have been living here three bitches, two Siamese cats, one of which is feeding three kittens, a languorous and interminable black tom, two dogs and two aboriginal cats. Of the thirteen, the three Parisian felines ignored the existence of the canine species, the sea and the countryside. The accord was miraculous, in the narrow human sense we give the word. A prolonged, definitive, olfactory investigation suffices for the cats. The bitches, warned in a few words, exhibited the dissimulation and politeness we expected of them; and anyway, the nursing cat taught them, in a few seconds of terrifying apparition, that a nursing cat is the equivalent of a horde of demons. A pair of finches, occupied—counter to all tradition and probability in the month of August—with a nest where two unfeathered fledglings cheep, nested above the front door and showed themselves not wanting in cordiality, fluttering above our heads, gathering provender in flight, picking it up from between the dogs' paws, and chirping under the noses of the cats, offended and scornful at such presumption. As for us, the two-legged ones, we are still delighted by the charming and preposterous sight of a terrace where cats and dogs slumber in the hours of heat, hovered over by trusting finches. Such peace is dear to us and we cannot refrain from stroking this one, congratulating the other on its perfect urbanity, cradling the long tom in our lap whence it slips away, stretching, spread out, like an almost fluid putty. . . . Then the scene suddenly changes. The congratulated cat opens a dragon's mouth and punishes some innocent; the bitch one is stroking bristles, the hair of its back like a sole's backbone, and chases the smallest dog from its shade; a Siamese, drowsy till now, crawls in strategic demonstration against a low-perched finch; the other Siamese explodes into oaths, treating the tom as a child-stealer. . . . Everything is spoiled, the sentimental sky of our earthly paradise is darkened, because we have just cast there the demoralizing shadow, the unlucky hand of the master, of him who leads animals astray, discloses his love and jealousy, and would see himself without rival in their once pure hearts.

Beauties

Madame P., too much of a beauty, disfigures herself. Another beauty, Romanian this time, kills herself because of the first wrinkle. Man, be satisfied, be glorious, both sacrifice themselves for you. Of the two victims the most naïve is certainly the one who bathed her perfect features in sulphuric acid. A lot of good it has done her, as they say. All she can hope for now is not to hear, falling from ungrateful cherished lips, the word once heard by a beautiful would-be suicide who had just placed a bullet in her shoulder and was not dying: 'Imbecile. . . .'

Whenever a woman tries to remedy the inconveniences of an amorous passion she either makes a mistake or else swaps an evil for a disaster. She is beloved by fate alone and loses all in sinning against it. Let us suppose that Madame P. had continued to dazzle and desolate her rivals with her unique splendour, to wound a jealous and madly infatuated husband to the heart. Would the set-up have ended in drama? I am sure it would, but in what I dare describe as a normal drama: the husband's suicide, a duel between the said husband and a suspected lover. All that is within the tradition, I might even say the banality, of fierce and ordinary love. 'I'll kill you,' threatened a jealous woman. 'That's your affair,' her husband very sensibly replied. Nothing guaranteed Madame P. the development of predestined tragedy.

But, forgoing the four or five gestures consistent with the logic of her life, she chose the monstrous challenge that confounds the simple issues and fixes the unhappy woman in a deadlock, disfigured and left to contemplate the prospects for her love.

It's nothing to be born ugly. Sensibly, the ugly woman comes to terms with her ugliness and exploits it as a grace of nature. To become ugly means the beginning of a calamity, self-willed most of the time. In destroying her beauty Madame P. shows that she counts on the nobility of soul of a hitherto tormented spouse. 'Now he'll be happy,' she says. Alas! If once he loved her material form, he may have forgotten long since that she was the most beautiful woman in the world. Obsessed, on the other hand, he thought only of this beauty. He cursed it, abused it, blamed it as the source of all his troubles. Poor man, what is he left with now? The right to display, peacefully now, the being of whose treasure he once wished to be the sole possessor? Allow me a moment to consider this widower, this rich man driven mad by overflowing possessions. According to the newspapers, he is 'inconsolable'. He implores the medical profession to restore his reason for living, his reason for hating, for suspicion. If he has any charity, will he not cry inwardly 'If only she were dead!' For already he can see further than the rash woman, he is capable of picturing the course of future events, the sudden sleep of all the passions, and the appearance, in a setting still redolent of impassioned wrongs and sensual conflict, of courtesy, disinterestedness, kind attentions, all those virtues that would have waited patiently to be ushered in by mature age. . . .

That's enough pity to offer the one who has not suffered the irreparable effects of vitriol. Well, to whom shall I extend it then? To the self-burnt? Excuse me, but I cannot. I cannot concede that a proprietor has the right to lay waste his own property. Madame P. puts me in mind of the stupid whim of defiance that finished off Felicity, a Normandy farmer. Felicity governed and worked to exhaustion her nephew, a man of all work, who used to grumble unendingly 'Oh, Aunt, if only I could see you in the well!' One day Felicity cried impatiently 'Like this?' and jumped into the well. The nephew married the pretty little servant-girl. . . . But this anecdote is not intended as a fable.

The other beauty who, this week, celebrated her fiftieth birthday with a very successful suicide, deserves that I should think of her with regret, if simply to blame her for knowing only how to be beautiful. The fear of ageing, a commonplace neurosis, does not usually wait for age and spares neither sex. Mlle de V., aged twenty-six, once confided to me that it ruined her appetite and sleep in advance. This was doing things on the grand scale, prematurely to prospect the feminine hell peopled, once age has come, by so many 'beautiful Mesdames So-and-so'. In contrast with such frenzy, the deceased Romanian might have taken the path of so many pharmaceutical establishments, violet-ray laboratories, laboratories for blue light, dyeing, massage and surgery, that she would never have found the time to quit this world. But this proud woman doubtless lived a withdrawn life, imprisoned with two equally pitiless spies—her mirror and her lover. In which of these two did she witness her declining image for the first time?

I was talking about her to a friend, a spruce quinquagenarian, who judged her with light peremptoriness. 'Pooh! These are a foreigner's ideas. We French women, we shall never lack for occupation once love is over. We have the family, scandalmongering, the love-affairs of others, and greed.'

I nodded assent, reflecting on a recent glimpse of two women who had been beautiful, celebrated and rivals. The one, hardly aged at all, blowzy and gluttonous in front of a plate of Spanish *puchero*; the other, all claws and velvet like a cat's paw, her cheek still smooth, her light blue eyes blazing with eternal malice. . . .

Offspring

In Germany a butcher kills them, salts them and eats them. As for us, we buy and sell them, put them down and take them up again, deck them out and exchange them. From time to time some child is discovered hidden away in a cupboard in the midst of darkness and filth; every month brings its news-item of a child branded with a poker, bruised with blows, starving; public opinion, represented by neighbours on the same floor, brings it to the attention of justice after an interval that is usually a long one, for public opinion, scrupulous, likes to garner the evidence in minute detail. . . . To repeat the expression of a small girl I know, 'It's becoming quite impossible to be a child!'

We now have a more or less complete list of the Galou pseudo-offspring. These, as it happens, seem hardly to have suffered. If one or two were lost, it was from inadvertence and not from brutality. But what can one think of the mother who handed them over, in all propriety, to a monomaniac of maternity? We are horrified by the pale and shameful little renunciatory contract drafted by one of the defaulting mothers; but it's because we don't read often enough those newspaper pages where the traffic in children publishes its advertisements between the bargain piano and the 'twice worn' fur coat. It is there that an authentic marquis, whose days are numbered, refuses to die out altogether and wants his name to survive him by ennobling some cherished commoner's head. There that a family without issue cannot contemplate sterile old age.

Rights, clandestine cares, are exchanged for a little money; it is not a matter of enormous sums, for the secretive adoption is one of the rare commodities whose cost has not quintupled since the war. . . . How easy it all is, how romantic, inadmissible and every-day! Every kind of traffic seems authorized when it's a matter of suppressing or banishing an inconvenient child. In my own local cemetery a pretty truncated column marks the place of a new-born who lived for a week. It was the child of a lady—a young lady, rather—who came to stay in Puisaye for three months, heavy and ravishingly beautiful, and went away lighter, having delivered her fruit to a local doctor. The doctor died too, but much later on, after having added to his medical rank the ephemeral title of Minister of Finance. But who ever knew the name of the beautiful sinner?

I date from a time, I come from an area, where the traffic in Parisian 'foster-children' provided an income for nurses, wet or dry. My elder brother, a country doctor, used to take me on his rounds and I could guess, from his sombre expression, when the time came for his tour of inspection of the Parisian infants. For one child who flourished in his rural squalor, ten cost us laughter and appetite just to look at them. We would arrive without warning to find the little patient alone in the farm building, swaddled in its cradle, dummy in mouth and eyes black with flies. Or else it cried endlessly, given over to the care of a four-year-old. One of these, at eight months, was nourished on lard, cabbage soup and cider, like a grown-up. 'But what he likes best,' his nurse proudly assured us, 'are gooseberries. Ah, *he* doesn't want to go back to Paris !'

And he did not go back, and for good reason. . . .

Brittany, Puisaye, it was the same hecatomb. Did I not this week come across, at an antiquary's at Saint-Servan, a sturdy piece of Louis XIII furniture, a squat cabinet, a sort of deep sideboard with two thick, hermetically closing doors. 'It was inside this,' said the merchant as he opened it, 'that they used to put small children—see, the two planks that made the cradle are still there—and then they were shut in and like that the parents could go to work in the fields without their little ones being eaten by the pigs.'

Have the last twenty-five or thirty years altered the fate of these foster-children? Surely. First, there are not so many children now. And then, nowadays, they don't wait for a child to come into the world before getting rid of it. A simplification that resorts to criminal surgery and that has abolished the familiar picture that used to dishonour—for instance—a certain railway station in the open fields where the nurses, back from Paris, well provided with squalling infants, money and alcohol, used to take a snack. . . . Prostrate or feverish new-born infants, the sour odour of milk churned up by the train, new swaddling-clothes, a dirty pink ribbon, a coarse black hand rocking the basket that sheltered four or five little ones higgledy-piggledy. . . .

As a small girl I was scared by these kidnappers, who were for the most part no more than simple or greedy peasant women. But my sensitive elder brother lost, in their context, courage and inclination for his profession. My mother, loving protector of all nascent life, did her best to save these still secret children. On two occasions she took girl-mothers into her service, saying no more to them than 'Lift up your corset now, my girl'. Poor morality? That was the narrow provincial judgment on this morality, too elevated for it.

Nowadays it is the child-welfare officer or the eugenist who provides for the most urgent cases. Given the dearth of French children, France may well take nurselings from no matter where, and in the manner of the strange Madame Galou. It is not difficult to collect bastards and orphans. It is less easy to protect against their own parents the lamentable number of little Poil-de-Carotte who sigh : 'Everyone can't be an orphan. . . .' Between the spoilt middle-class baby—unhappy autocrat who divides two doting families the better to reign over them—and the little skinny martyr, fodder for news-items, there is room for more than one kind of unhappy child, beginning with those households where divorce assumes the periodicity, and almost the frequency, of a cure. Vandérem will tell you that these children, whether well brought up or spoiled, can pass for the happiest creatures in the world. Nevertheless, for lack of love and instinctive attachment, these same children feel unstable and anxious and would regret, had they ever known it, the patriarchal peace of the Orient, the harem that witnesses the growth of the mingled laughing sons of Fatima and daughters of Aïscha. They cast a happier shadow than do the obstetric clinics, those pink-washed walls and the columns of the enclosed patio, at the centre of which a dreaming urchin, leaving his play, leans randomly against a female knee or checks his impulse at some breast which, though not having borne his growing weight, is nonetheless maternal. . . .

Mausoleums

The friends of Marie Bashkirtseff* are up in arms and reveal that decay threatens the tomb of one who was a restless young woman, glory-struck and a peripatetic invalid. I see no harm in vigilant friends scraping off the moss and restoring the stone, though I prefer those tombs that are loaded with unrestrained vegetation and spared the rake. I respect the devoted care of the hands that clean the crown of pearls, change the water in the little vase and

* Marie Bashkirtseff (1860–84), the Russian-born author of a remarkable *journal intime,* in which she records her struggle against the consumption that finally killed her.

rub down the engraved marble; but, in my view, these are attentions better suited to a little villa for the living than a chapel for
the dead.

I haven't recently visited the pleasant cemetery at Passy, where
rest the famous dead. The last time I was there was when I
repaired to the tomb of Renée Vivien* and then I was accompanied by one of the most lively of the living—I refer to Annie de
Pène. She showed me over the garden, pleasant in all seasons but
enhanced by the clear autumn weather.

She traversed the narrow paths with familiarity, picking off a
dried-up rose, rearranging a bouquet with those marvellous hands
of hers that touched everything with assurance, made fruit and
vegetables more appetizing, could break a branch and throw a log
on the fire. Annie pursed her lips at Renée's tomb, found fault
with some faded violets, and laid beside the dead flowers some
fresh violets she had brought. She never stopped talking but did
me the honours of the enclosure and named the inmates as if it
were a drawing-room. 'That's Marie Bashkirtseff over there, this
is that charming little Henriot who died of burns. . . . I tell you,
Colette, this is the best sort of cemetery for a woman. The others
are big, crowded, it's a scrimmage! But here, my word, it's the
devil to get in, you have to know someone. . . .' Her gaiety was no
insult to the peace of the dead and we spoke of Renée Vivien as
if she might have been waiting for us, five minutes from there, at
her home in the avenue du Bois. Annie shook her stubborn
Norman forehead in irritation. 'Finished at thirty, what stupidity!
How can one live eating so little, feeding on raw fish and grapes,
hiding from the daylight behind stained-glass windows in the glow
of three brown wax candles: Renée Vivien would have done
better to eat my stuffed chicken or my creamed haddock. But
perhaps a poet can't eat stuffed chicken without risking ceasing to
be a poet. I know nothing about it; I'm afraid of poets. And yet
she was a charming creature, this tall fair girl who's asleep under
the violets and who never discussed her poetic gift. I must say, I
prefer invalids who don't tell you about their diseases!'

---

* Renée Vivien (1877–1909), pseudonym of Pauline Tarn, born in London
of an English father and an American mother. She lived mostly in Paris and
wrote sensuous verse influenced by Baudelaire.

It's true, Renée Vivien never spoke of her 'disease'. She did not recite verses, demanded neither praise nor criticism. A foreigner, she thought and wrote our language with purity, but she might have found it hard to comprehend those words that still vibrate in Marie Bashkirtseff's underground chamber : 'To succeed . . . to arrive. . . .' Yet even Renée Vivien left a body of work.

I think that her soul was like her face, which was fair, coiffed with fine flaxen, golden hair, and childlike from the forehead to the small English mouth. Laughing brown eyes, a kind of mobile artlessness, kept her countenance ever young. I used to say to her 'Renée, you've only the body of a writer', teasing her about her long, long, insubstantial, stooping body. It was what she wanted, this long thin body, ever more frail, ever thinner, and she foolishly went without eating.

I don't think that anyone has had much to say about her dark, sumptuous and changing apartment. At the back of the courtyard of the same building Robert d'Humières sometimes inhabited a bachelor establishment, ornamented with exotic souvenirs and a white cat. Apart from a few Buddhas and the antique instruments of the music-room, all the furniture moved and changed mysteriously at Renée Vivien's. A collection of Persian gold coins gave way to jade, were replaced by a collection of butterflies and rare insects. She wandered about among tottering marvels and displayed them with an exile's pleasure : 'I can't find my new Buddha! Marie, Marie, where have you put the Buddha I got yesterday?' How charming she was, one sometimes saw her as the farouche priestess of some strange sentimental cult! Towards her guests she behaved with the eagerness of a well-brought-up young girl, watching them dine while nibbling at grilled almonds and fruit. She also had a young girl's sudden blush and a liking for tall stories and over-strong liqueurs. She cried like a child, then laughed one night when, overcome by shadow and unable to eat beneath a canopy of sombre hangings starred with occasional candles, I brought along and set down by my plate an offensive, inadmissible and indispensable paraffin lamp worth five francs seventy-five.

I may not seem to evoke a poetess, gravely devoted to her art. It was just that she worked unobtrusively, with little noise. At

Nice I often surprised her sitting on the edge of a cane divan, writing verses on her knees. She would get up with a guilty air and excuse herself : 'I've just finished. . . .' Even in death she remains far removed from her Slav neighbour, anxious for fame, who would have given ten years of her delicate and burning youth for a sprig of official laurel. Beautiful and young, early of the elect, it may be that they lean over the bar of Heaven to see what we preserve of theirs. So let us give to each what they loved on earth; let us restore the tomb of Marie Bashkirtseff and, for Renée Vivien, let us encourage the grass, the viburnum that climbs and hides her name, the wild violet. . . .

Newspapers

For anyone who spends more than six weeks on a miraculously inviolate shore, with no sound but the battering of the angry sea, the faint, silky ripping of the calm tides, the mewing of the gulls and the plaintive note of the red-foot, reading the newspapers becomes astonishing. 'An hour's delirium' is what we call the period after the arrival of the postman here.

We are not scared off immediately—Paris keeps up with us for a long while when we leave it in July. A grey mist of crimes, thefts, infanticides and embezzlements, spreads over the summer newspapers, passes before our surfeited, unresting gaze. The long columns resemble provincial streets, empty and silent, where a sudden echo repeats the brief explosion of a revolver-shot, perhaps a single cry. It's July, the time of rejuvenation of our senses, surprised and exiled to the point when, in the early days, holding a newspaper stretched and flapping in the breeze, we say : 'Another woman cut into eight pieces, what a bore. . . . Aren't they done with their parricides and stories of kidnapped children?' But we call out at the top of our voice, arms raised : 'Come and see, come quickly! The shadow of the cloud is violet on the sea! And there's a rose on the rose-bush! Run, run, or you won't see this animal, I don't know its name, I've never seen anything like it, it's got feet like a grasshopper and a golden head, quickly!'

Gradually equilibrium is restored and ecstasy becomes habit. Replete, equable, dedicated to physical enthusiasm and mental serenity, every day our life becomes better and further removed from what it was in our urban epoch. The fine weather, the lunar months, the harvests, the colour and caprice of the storms, the prognostications of the birds, the quivering desire for sociability expressed by the wild game, normal life in fact, bathes us and we live, initiate and at peace, at the heart of its miracles. Beautiful refuge, where we discover in the distance what we have abandoned! A single day, a single glance, do not suffice. The rock fissure, filled with sea-water, does not reveal its treasures all at once. Only gradually does our persistence fathom the depth of a glacial green, carpeted with sea-wrack, discern the crab's moving jaws and the living beard of the shrimps among the delicate weed, the agonizing drama of a small conger-eel cut in two by a crab. . . .

Little by little, having laid the newspaper aside, we return to it; and little by little the phantasmagoria and horror of daily life in a hundred civilized places reaches us. At five hundred kilometres from Paris the unaccustomed smell of newly printed paper stands for fever, ambition, ferocity, often macabre comedy. As we read, a drowsy naïveté evokes in us a loud exclamation, a communal indignation. There's reason for it.

'Did you see about this stolen necklace? Yes, a necklace worth five millions, isn't that enough to tempt the Devil? And did you see where a prisoner and a warder conspired to rob the prison safe? Oh . . . it's outrageous, damn it!'

Friends arriving from Paris and stopping by listen to us indulgently. It's true that we question them as if they've left a Gehenna where people kill one another, where the 'flics' hurl themselves at the heels of men who flee, scattering pearls and wads of banknotes in their tracks. The newspaper, all surface news, no longer has a bite for these crusted city-dwellers whom we shall come to resemble after the equinoctial tides. But my word, what a harvest in one week! In seven days God allows himself less vagaries than his own creatures. '*A train runs into a sandal factory. Three jewellers, terrified at the sight of a cotton-wool bomb, hand over three hundred thousand francs to a miscreant in a hold-up. A business employee slashes a woman passer-by. An engaged couple go for a walk in the bois de Vincennes; they are assaulted by three false policemen who ill-treat the young man and abuse the young girl. A lawyer and his mistress fight a revolver duel. A seventy-five-year-old father is thrown out by his children and left on a chair by the kerbside. Fifty-seven millions, left in a car for an hour, disappear . . .*', etc., etc.

How the fate of these robbed, slashed, ill-treated individuals excites our curiosity and compassion! How well we understand the word, reduced to the singular, that the peasants use. Contemptuous of any political implication, there are many of them who still speak of '*the* newspaper', with no other specification of the invasive, perturbing gazette. Let us admit that a facile technique, a concise lyricism, almost everywhere inform the news-item, jewel of the front page, the guts of what, typically, is called the 'body' of the paper. Humour smiles there, among the hecatombs. Eros juggles there with tibiae.

Perhaps what is lacking at the sessions of the League of Nations, so that the fate of the world might compete in interest far afield with the most recent tortures of Biribi, the disappearance of a sempstress and the assassination of a sexagenarian by a pretty young woman, perhaps what is lacking is the ingenious, enthusiastic, tragic, pseudo-naïve bard who edits here, there, everywhere, the news of the day. I picture him, this Proteus, given a free hand at the Geneva Conference and giving all his attention to a jaundiced diplomatic smile, producing for the public, like so many impassioned articles, the chain and seal of Monsieur X. . . , the monogrammed portfolio of Monsieur Z. . . . A light touch with the colour of a capital execution, a hint of the Assize Court, what success. . . .

But the protocols of Geneva are edited by upright career journalists, by secretly ardent politicians who conscientiously 'play the game'. It is not these we shall ask to relate, with due extravagant seriousness, the adventure of the American multi-millionaire who sees his two daughters elope with two of his servants. Is it just our natural rusticity? Is it the talent of our specialist colleagues, and the sickly satanism they know how to impart to fifteen inoffensive lines? I don't know; but we are thrilled and stunned to learn that an 'exclusive' clan of Massachusetts millionaires has gone into mourning because of the double misalliance, and that the father of these two rebellious near thirty-year-olds declines henceforward 'to be seen in public'.

Wings

It is beyond dispute that I can fly in dreams. You too. I add 'in dreams' because my efforts, like yours, have not succeeded—by a sound, a strangled sigh—in crossing the frontier that separates the two worlds, only one of which we designate, arbitrarily, as 'real'. I can cross a valley; pivot, to turn, on one or other of my flying arms; and swoop down, head first, feet raised to gain speed, then straighten my trunk to regain the horizontal for climbing or landing. And how I sport with the wind, in this entire universe! Entire, because it possesses its pale day-star, its nights less dark than earthly nights, its plants, its population of the loved dead, of the keenly staring unknown, its animal life especially. The most recent animal I encountered there dates from last week, for the full moon, which sends cats delirious, authorizes my brief visits to this boundless continent. A black feline, as big as a Great Dane, was waiting to fight with me and we fought gravely, not in frenzy but as if for sport, while meantime I noticed the shape of its eyes, more horizontal than those of cats, and the particular pink of its mouth, opened whenever it wished to frighten or bite me. A very real animal, in fact, whose contact and appearance inspired my dreaming double with no more than normal curiosity, the normal desire to vanquish a strange animal, and the confused ill-formulated conceit of bringing off a victory *up there*: '*They* will be pleased with it; I'll display it to *them* as if it had always been mine. . . .' But it was the same with the beautiful black feline as with that little tortoise with the bird's head, so friendly, that climbs in the trees and cheeps . . . you know. No, you don't know. The bird-tortoise remained on the far side of the gate with the great black feline, the intelligent sociable serpent, the dog that silently regards me and puts his hand in mine, the man who holds out an open notebook which I never have the time to read. . . .

Thanks, no doubt, to my perfect digestion, animals and people in my exclusive nocturnal empire are courteous and peaceable, even in combat. The flights that carry me over a familiar valley of dark fir-trees do not break my bones and I land, instead of falling, in the middle of the bed after one of those jolts as severe as any earthquake. Did the same flight haunt the dreams of a Maneyrol, a Barbot, a Simonet, of all those who seek the dream-remembered motorless soaring, the everlasting wing? An aviator obsessed with gliders assured me that, while it takes our wingless species long study to control an aeroplane, an ancient science intervenes when it comes to the glider in which man progresses as if seated in the midst of an enchanted cloud, drunk with a newly recognized but ancient gift, in the newly conquered air. I can well believe it. All is marvellous that astounds senses as deadened and mutilated as ours. Flight exists for us only in dream, the complete being is he who sleeps and is newly born, for the new-born swims at birth like the sightless kitten and puppy. But its human condition holds it back and denies it one more element; two months later the 'little man' can no longer swim.

I ruminate on our downfall, lying stretched out on a shorn meadow where the seeds of the last dandelions rise, ballasted by their minuscule oblong fruit, tufted with spun silver. They progress slowly, visible for a long time against the misty blue of the sky; they stop and rest in the air without descending. It is also the season for the thistle-seed to emigrate. This flies in a different fashion, an iridescent hedgehog rolling on the tip of its bristles, descending the length of an invisible slope, climbing an aerial hillock. Two cormorants cleave the sky, not too high for me to fail to distinguish the angled articulation of the outer third of their wings, which constitute their private mystery of living mechanism.

They have arrived with the high tide and only pass over us to where the long estuary of the Rance beckons. Our faithful sparrow-hawks do not need these folded wings to execute, in a flash, the path of their patrol from Saint-Malo to Cancale, from Cancale to the nest which I respect; propellants hidden in their widespread, unmoving wings bear them up against the strong wind. . . . Flight, abandonment to the lost element, thirst that even the aeroplane cannot satisfy, torment of the creature, stretched crucified on the earth, who lifts his gaze on high. . . .

My tame finch does not concern himself with the sky. He lives like the hens and runs about in mouse disguise to terrify the cats. He runs, picks up the crumbs thrown to him, climbs the stairs using his feet, and sadistically acts the cripple. Cripple? Ah, if he only wished. . . . He does wish sometimes and climbs with a jeering cry into his modest finch's heaven, his sky, so low, informed with earthly smokes and smells. Little fawn wings, feeble beating apparatus of a sedentary bird. . . .

September gathers the swallows and sees the summer butterflies perish. Deflowered of their vulcans, peacock and tortoise-shell butterflies, the ground-lilac and the yellow broom have lost their most beautiful and quivering petals. But out of the mauve and yellow bouquet that remains something winged still launches itself : the venturesome spider leaves its web, casts itself off at the end of a silken cable, and rises borne by the wind. . . .

Back to School

They're going back. Their savages' feet, brown and hardened, re-experience the weight of the great shoes we have thoughtfully studded and strengthened with nails. A pair of good 'everyday shoes' for adolescents is as weighty as a shackle and our ballasted children frolicked with a shorter stride during those last recreations that served as dress-rehearsals before reassembly.

I was not moved by pity for my high-school girl, who executes the same gay dance on the threshold of her jail, whether coming or going. Certainly the schools of Paris and its surrounds welcome back, as boarders, many a strapping young woman like her, who will not go without either park or bathing. Neat, hair cut like a well-tended lawn, in pink aprons, it is a pretty posy of children that I run across at any time beneath the trees of Saint-Germain. They are well-conducted and their somewhat boyish vivacity is not altogether devoid of affectation. 'Once is not a habit,' said my own prisoner to me one day, 'I treated myself to a hair-wave.' From acquaintance with her best friends it seems to me that they soon learn to make prompt decisions, to run risks, and to take responsibility for their follies. My daughter's pocket-book notes various desiderata :

Buy writing-paper
Soap, toilet-water
A waterproof hat I've no need for: but people look
askance if one goes for a walk without a hat.
Ask Mama if I can become a Jewess.

I assented to writing-paper, soap and lotion, even the oilskin hat, without a murmur. But on the question of apostasy I allowed myself a brief inquiry :

'Why do you want to become a Jewess?'

'Oh, it's not that I'm keen on it, but you know, at school they're nearly all Jews, so it seems rather like a uniform. . . .'

Roses on the wall, sunny pavilions, musical scales and trills of laughter . . . I'm well aware that this unclouded picture of boarding-school life is not the same everywhere. Gloomy colleges still exist. There is, especially, the extraordinary and inexcusable lagging of the provinces behind Paris in the matter of boarding-schools for boys.

One worries sentimentally over them and I know that every year well-meaning propaganda accuses the boarding system of all manner of disgrace and crime. This year, however, firmer and more numerous voices are raised in its defence in Paris and its periphery. It's from the provinces that the angry denunciations come, directed against the length of the classes, the total neglect of hygiene, and the incurable gloom that shrouds the decrepit buildings where our scattered sons languish. Optimists when they have daughters, our mothers sing the praises and advantages of the boarding system; pessimists where sons are concerned, other mothers malign it and bewail their fate from the heart of the ancestral home, bereft of its greatest pride, its young masculine ornament.

Eternal weakness of one sex for the other! I happen to know five very French families with but a single blossom—I mean that the five couples have each produced a single girl. It's said that the small English girl is unsurpassed in beauty. But it's my view that a pretty little French girl, well loved and of good carriage, has few rivals. My five little princesses know how to use their charm. Family life revolves around them, though with difficulty at times since their parents work. Five sensible mothers insist that their daughters' moral and physical hygiene demands a boarding-school near Paris to ensure the children's comfort and their parents' peace of mind. But five fathers, jealous as lovers, selfish as husbands, resist. What, give up the brief radiant encounter with 'la petite', the dinner-table chit-chat, the evening kiss, the sound of cantering feet? Never! Each of these impassioned fathers defends his treasure with such convinced ardour that I think of La Palférine's remark: 'Cut Claudine's hair? I'd rather see her dead!'

Is boarding-school a prison? 'It was in our time' many a man affirms who is over twenty-five, and almost all who are past forty. I don't doubt their sincerity and I am reminded of two older brothers, formerly entrusted to the College at Auxerre. Dirty, emaciated, devoured by fleas in summer, swollen with chilblains in winter, they endured their torment in dumb hatred. But this refers to a remote period, the period when I saw my sister, too, return from her boarding-school in the provincial capital changed, dispirited and miserable. It was the captivity of these three older ones that decided my liberty. 'Oh no, not for her!' murmured my mother as she looked at me. . . .

The concept of the boarding system is probably a monstrous one. But its application seems inevitable in future. For it is important, in too many cases, to remove the child from what an ignorant sentimentality still calls 'the warm and peaceful atmosphere of the home', in fact the narrow incubator which approximates the elbows and foreheads of two or three generations, the one the issue of the other, the one often the enemy of the other.

Nowadays the private life of parents is less mysterious for the child than the book one shuts away in a library; and how many couples constrain themselves, in front of the child, to the respectable lie, the pretended harmony? Is it certain that boarding-school corrupts a child? One may well wager that it will corrupt him less, and that our offspring will rather derive from fathers and mothers whose bonds are trivial a precocious apprenticeship, the bitterest, in all that destroys security, a sense of permanence, and faith. Whatever we may think, our children do not change; but we seem determined to diminish ourselves before them. Adult stupidity and inertia crack up the father as a pal and the mother as a friend, innovations prone to determine the son as judge and the daughter as rival.

'Away with the corrupting promiscuity of the boarding-schools!' I say the same as you, honest reformers. But I am not sure that whispered conversations in a study corner, books or newspapers passed from desk to desk, spoil and stain the precious fruit more than do your homely lessons of conjugal quarrelling, conversations in hinted words, the negligent looseness of our morals, in fact the spectacle of your fine adult existence as taken in by two large unfathomable eyes, by two small ears that shudder at what they understand, that retain the sound of an insulting word, a servile prayer, or a slamming door.